7.2 Red Tape

- Practice past modals: Speculation & deduction
- Talk about problems with bureaucracy

a

b

c

Speaking & Vocabulary: Bureaucracy

1 Look at images a–c. Where do you think the people are? What is happening? How do they feel? Why?

2 a Work in pairs. Read the definition and answer the questions.

> **red tape** the documents and procedures associated with bureaucratic systems such as applying for a passport, a bank account or registering a complaint

1 What's the connection between the definition and image c?
2 What do you think the people are lining up for? Choose from the options in the box. Use a dictionary to help you.

application for a driver's license
enrollment form   formal complaint form
job application   tax return
visa or passport application

b What documents might be necessary for the procedures in 2a? Can you add any more to the list in the box?

a birth certificate   an ID card   a medical certificate
a passport   proof of address   a resident's certificate

3 Work in groups. Discuss the questions.

- Have you had to fill out any official forms recently?
- Was it a complicated procedure? Did you have to provide any extra documents? If so, which ones?
- Do you often have to deal with paperwork like this?
- What problems do people usually face when dealing with bureaucracy, in your experience?

Listening

1 7.2 Listen to a talk about how to deal with bureaucracy. Answer the questions.

1 What does the acronym RACE stand for?
2 Which two images a–c are referred to as examples?

2 a Listen again and take notes on what Sanjay says about each word in the acronym in 1.

b Work in pairs. Compare your notes. What mistakes did the people make in the two situations?

3 Do you disagree with any of Sanjay's tips? Which ones? Why? Are there any suggestions you would add?

Grammar

1 a Look at sentences a–e from Transcript 7.2. Underline the modal verbs.

a He might have forgotten an important document.
b He could have made a mistake on his form.
c He couldn't have read the form carefully.
d He must have found something suspicious in his case.
e He may not have fulfilled all the requirements.

b Answer the questions about sentences a–e in 1a.

1 Are they talking about the past or the present?
2 Is the speaker certain that what he says is true/not true?

2 Complete 1–5 in the GRAMMAR PANEL with sentences a–e from 1a.

3 Rewrite bold phrases 1–6 using past modals.

I'm writing about a package that was sent from Australia a month ago. (1)**I'm sure something has gone wrong** because it still hasn't arrived. (2)**There's no way I missed the mailman** because there's always someone in the house. (3)**It's impossible that it got lost** because packages are tracked electronically. (4)**Perhaps the mailman delivered** it to the wrong address. Or (5)**it's possible he left it** with a neighbor. I reported the problem a week ago, but (6)**it's possible you haven't tracked** down the package yet.

4 Work in pairs. Look at the image of the car. What do you think has happened? Use the ideas in the box and your own ideas.

break down · have an accident · park illegally · pay a parking fine · have a valid license

The driver might have had an accident.

Past Modals: Speculation & Deduction

We use *must/could/might/may/couldn't* + *have* + past participle to speculate and make deductions about the past.

Uses

A speculation about a past event or situation we...	
1 are sure happened.	(1) ....
2 think possibly happened.	(2) .... *He may have brought the wrong form.* (3) ....
3 think possibly didn't happen.	(4) .... *He might not have known about the law.*
4 are sure didn't happen.	(5) ....

See page 146 for grammar reference and more practice.

Pronunciation: Past modals

1 a 7.3 Listen and circle the words you hear.

1 I suppose I could *put / have put* my keys in your bag.
2 Her parents might not *let / have let* her come!
3 Careful! You could *hurt / have hurt* yourself!
4 Don't worry, he may not *have come / come*.
5 They couldn't *have closed / closed* the pool. Lots of people go there!

b How is *have* pronounced in the sentences in 1a?

2 Work in pairs. Take turns reading out loud one of the options for the sentences in 1a. Listen and identify the option you hear.

Speaking

1 Think of a time you had a problem or misunderstanding in one of the situations in the box.

with a gas / water / electric company
at the bank / post office
at a passport office / embassy / tax office

Prepare notes about...
- what happened
- why you think it happened
- how you felt
- how you resolved the situation.

2 a Work in groups of three. Talk about each problem, using your notes from 1.

b Share ideas about why each situation happened.
- For your problem, do you agree with your group's ideas about your situation?
- For other people's problems, do you think they resolved the situation well? Why/Why not?

- LEARN ABOUT CROWD BEHAVIOR
- DISCUSS TEAM-BUILDING ACTIVITIES

SPEAKING

1 a Work in pairs. Rank statements a–d according to how strongly you agree with them.

1 = strongly agree 2 = agree 3 = not sure
4 = disagree 5 = strongly disagree

a .... I hate crowds. I usually avoid going to busy shopping malls, large concerts or sporting events.

b .... I love big cities. I love the buzz and excitement of a crowd.

c .... I could never live alone or work from home. I like being surrounded by people; I feel miserable by myself.

d .... We always go out in a large group. It's important to invite everyone; you can't leave anyone out.

b Work with another pair. Compare your responses in 1a. Then answer the questions about the last time you were in a crowd.

1 Where were you?
2 What were you doing?
3 How did you feel?
4 Did you enjoy the experience? Why/Why not?

READING

1 Read the definitions and answer the questions.

1 What's the connection between the definitions?
2 How do you think they relate to images a–d?

herd a group of animals of the same species that travel or are kept together

herd mentality the way that large numbers of people behave in the same way at the same time

2 a Read the article. What is the connection to images a–d?

b Match headings a–f to paragraphs 1–6.

a Safety in Numbers	....	d Anything for a Bargain	....
b Machines to the Rescue	....	e Follow your Neighbors	....
c The End of Mob Rule?	....	f The Smell of Success	....

3 a Complete statements 1–6 using your own words.

1 The writer didn't go into the department store because...
2 Starlings don't collide when they move in formation because...
3 Animals are safer in groups because...
4 A trucking company saved thousands of dollars by...
5 Robots can help people in disaster areas by...
6 Crowds are often unruly because people... rather than...

b Read the article again and check.

a

b

c

d

4 Work in pairs. Discuss the questions.

- Do you agree that people have a herd mentality? Why/Why not?
- In what situations do people behave badly in groups?
- Have you had a similar experience to the one in the department store? What happened? How did you feel?

VOCABULARY: Collective nouns

1 a Find the collective nouns in the box in the article in **READING 2a**. What do they describe?

crew flock gang herd horde mob pack swarm

b Work in pairs. Answer the questions.

1 Which nouns in **1a** usually describe a) people? b) birds? c) insects? d) mammals?
2 Which words can have a negative meaning? Why?

2 a Which of the words in **1a** can you use to describe 1–8?

1 cows	4 seagulls	7 dogs
2 soccer fans	5 criminals	8 sailors
3 bees	6 protestors	

b What is the largest group (of animals or people) you have seen? How did it make you feel?

SPEAKING

1 a Work in groups of four. Your team members in the company where you work are unhappy and do not work well together. You have decided to do a team-building activity.

Student A, turn to page 159.
Student B, turn to page 161.
Student C, turn to page 163.
Student D, turn to page 164.

b Work with a partner with the same role card from a different group. Discuss the advantages and disadvantages of your activity.

2 a Explain your activity to your group. Decide together which activity will be best for bringing the team together.

b Report back. Which activity did you choose? Why?

NOTICE BODY VERBS

We can also use these parts-of-the-body nouns as verbs:

elbow: *Everyone was elbowing one another out of the way.*
eye: *He eyed my dessert greedily.*
mouth: *She mouthed the words slowly.*

Herd Mentality

1

Last year I was standing outside a New York department store the day the sales started. As soon as the doors opened, a mob of shoppers rushed in. Everyone was elbowing one another out of the way. A gang of teenage girls started fighting over T-shirts. Even though I had waited over an hour, I couldn't bear to go in. I was disgusted to see people acting like animals. But recently I've realized that they weren't behaving like animals—quite the opposite, in fact.

2

Think of birds. In autumn, you see enormous flocks of starlings in an astonishing, natural display of formation flying. Thousands fly together, but they never collide. They move as a single organism. How does this happen? Peter Miller discusses it in his best-seller *The Smart Swarm*. He explains that each starling only watches the six birds closest to it. It tracks those birds at all times and copies their movements. This way, the birds keep moving as one large flock.

3

Staying in large groups keeps animals safe. Take a herd of reindeer. If there is a pack of wolves following the herd, it will be in danger. Wolves can hide from one reindeer, but if hundreds of reindeer are watching at the same time, one is bound to spot the predators. Alone, the reindeer are helpless, but together they are strong.

4

Miller describes how scientists are applying some of the principles of swarms to solve human problems. For example, a trucking company was inspired by a swarm of ants. When ants look for food, they leave chemicals called pheromones to record the most successful routes for finding food. The company created a computer model for routing its trucks inspired by the ants' behavior. This saved the company thousands of dollars.

5

Scientists have also developed search-and-rescue robots that work in the same way as ants. The robots work in disaster areas to map an affected area and transmit reliable information to rescue crews.

6

Miller also shows how we can learn to manage groups of people by studying animal behavior. In certain situations, such as at an airport, people develop a herd mentality. They all do the same thing, following the leader. Crowds are only intelligent if individual members act responsibly and make their own decisions. By observing animal movements, it may be possible to organize public spaces better and prevent crazy situations like the rush during sales. So next time you're fighting with hordes of shoppers, you'd better grab a copy of this book, alongside those designer sunglasses!

TUNE IN

1 Work in groups. Discuss the questions.

- Have you ever had a bus/flight/train canceled or seriously delayed? Why? What happened?
- What usually happens when a flight is delayed or canceled?
- What does the airline do for passengers?

2 **a** 7.4 Listen to a man complaining about a canceled flight. What three pieces of advice is he given?

b Listen again and correct false statements 1–6.

1 The man is at the airport information desk.
2 His flight will leave later this afternoon.
3 He's traveling alone.
4 He's booked another flight on his iPad.
5 He's traveling on business.
6 He'll have to pay for dinner.

FOCUS ON LANGUAGE

3 **a** Match sentence halves 1–8 to a–h to make expressions from the audio.

1 I want to know ....
2 The problem is ....
3 What are we supposed ....
4 Do you have any idea ....
5 I'm afraid that ....
6 All I'm asking ....
7 You should have ....
8 This isn't the ....

a to do now?
b for is a flight home.
c better plans in place.
d what's going on.
e how difficult that is?
f just isn't good enough!
g first time it's happened.
h no one's telling us anything.

b Check your answers in Transcript 7.4 on page 165.

4 Work in pairs. Choose two appropriate expressions from 3a to use in each situation 1–3.

Situation 1
Your bank has made several administrative errors with your personal information. When they correct one mistake, another one appears.

Situation 2
The service in a restaurant was terrible. You waited over an hour for your main course. The management says you don't have to pay the service charge, but you think they should discount more from the bill.

Situation 3
The train you are waiting for has been canceled due to bad weather. It was the last train of the day to your destination and now you are stranded.

"Sounding frustrated"

7.5 Listen to five sentences. How does the speaker sound? How do you know?

Look at Transcript 7.5 on page 164. Underline the words that the speaker says slowly and loudly.

Practice saying the sentences with the same intonation.

OVER TO YOU

5 **a** Work in pairs. Choose one of the situations in 4 to act out.

Student A
You are the customer. You are not happy with the help you are being offered.

Student B
You work for the company. You are trying to help the customer and offer suggestions.

b Switch roles and act out a different situation.

6 Report back to the class. Which situation was more successful? Did the company respond to your criticism? Why/Why not?

TUNE IN

1 **a** Work in groups. What signs do the images show? What problems are they trying to prevent? Do you think they will be effective?

b Do you have any of these problems in your local community? What other social problems are common?

2 7.6 Listen to two people discussing the issues in images a–d. Number the images in the order they are mentioned.

3 Listen again and answer the questions.

1 Where do the speakers work?
2 What idea do they have?
3 What are their opinions on graffiti?
4 What is a problem for people with children?
5 Why are noise, graffiti and dog waste not at the top of the list?

a

b

c

d

PREPARE FOR TASK

4 Work in pairs. Complete sentences 1–7. Then listen again and check.

1 What concerns me most is ………… .
2 Surely the top priority has to be ………… .
3 Something else that really bothers me is ………… .
4 We should focus on ………… more than ………… .
5 Another thing people feel strongly about is ………… ………… .
6 I think it should go at the ………… of the list.
7 So speeding is ………… of the list, followed by ………… , then ………… and dog waste last.

5 Look again at the phrases in 4.

1 Which three phrases can you use to say that something is most important?
2 Which two phrases can you use to say that something is less important?

6 Do you agree with the order the speakers decide on? Why/Why not?

TASK

7 **a** Work in pairs. List the social problems in your community. How do they affect people?

b Choose four problems. Work together to rank them in order of priority. Use the expressions in 4.

8 Work with another pair. Agree together on the top four problems and on a final ranking.

REPORT BACK

9 **a** In your groups of four, present your top four problems and their final ranking to the class.

The issue we feel most strongly about is vandalism…

b Discuss as a class.

- Did any group agree on the same four problems?
- Which problem was at the top of the most lists?
- What are the best suggestions for dealing with this problem?

→ Go to Review C, Unit 7, p. 102 → Go to Writing Bank 4, p. 154

8 Crime and Punishment

a

b

c

1 Work in pairs. Look at the images and answer the questions.

1 What crime does each one show?
2 Are these crimes common where you live?
3 Why do you think people commit these crimes?

2 a Work in pairs. Complete A in the KEY VOCABULARY PANEL. Use a dictionary to help you.

b 8.1 Listen to two conversations. Which two images do they relate to?

3 a Listen again and answer the questions.

1 What did Sarah see in the store?
2 Why do schoolchildren shoplift according to Sarah?
3 What's Jim's attitude toward shoplifting?
4 What's Alex doing?
5 Why is the woman annoyed with him?
6 What's the problem for the music industry?

b Which opinion in conversations 1 and 2 in the audio do you agree with most? Why?

d

4 a Work in pairs. Complete B and C in the KEY VOCABULARY PANEL. Use a dictionary to help you.

b Complete sentences 1–6 with the correct form of words from B or C.

1 Tim had to pay a huge .... for speeding.
2 Someone .... $200,000 from the bank.
3 One of my colleagues was .... with tax evasion, but he insisted it was a mistake.
4 She got .... for disorderly conduct on Friday night.
5 I think the penalty for murder should be life ....
6 Our managing director has been .... of fraud.

5 Work in groups. Discuss the questions.

- Which crimes are common in your country?
- What penalties are usually given? Do you agree with them?
- Has anyone you know been a victim of crime? If so, what happened?

KEY VOCABULARY

Crime

A Types of crime

- Put the words in the box in the correct column.

arson burglary fraud illegal file sharing kidnapping looting mugging murder rioting robbing shoplifting tax evasion terrorism trespassing vandalism

Against property	Against a person
arson	*kidnapping*

B Penalties

- Which crimes would the punishments in the box be appropriate for? Are there any that you think should not be used at all?

capital punishment community service corporal punishment a fine life in prison a prison sentence

C Collocations

- Complete collocations 1–6 with the words in the box.

arrested a bank a crime (not) guilty money murder

1 steal ....
2 rob ....
3 commit ....
4 get .... for (trespassing)
5 charge someone with ....
6 find someone .... of (arson)

- Think of two other words you can use with the verbs in 1–3.

NOTICE *STEAL/ROB*

We use *steal* + the thing that is taken. We use *rob* + the person or place it is taken from:

She stole my bag. They stole $1,000.

She robbed me. They robbed the bank.

SPEAKING & READING

1 Work in pairs. Look at the images. They both show public humiliation being used as a form of punishment. Do you think this kind of punishment can be effective? Why/Why not?

2 **a** Read the online article about "shame punishment" and the comments that follow. How does the writer of the article feel about public humiliation? How do the writers of the two comments feel about it?

b Read the article and comments again. Match sections 1–6 to topics/questions a–f.

a In favor of "shame punishment" ....
b A fairer type of punishment? ....
c The return of "shame punishment" ....
d Are things better than in the Middle Ages? ....
e Arguments against "shame punishment" ....
f Punishment in the past ....

a

3 Work in pairs. Compare your answers in 2b. Then answer the questions.

1 What three arguments are given in support of "shame punishment"?
2 What three arguments are given against it?

4 Work in groups. Discuss the questions.

- Do you think Andrew Perry's actions were fair? Why/Why not?
- Which of the comments (5 and 6) do you agree with more? Why?

b

News | Sport | Comment | Culture | Business | Money | Life & style | Travel | Environment | TV | Blogs | Data | Mobile | Offers | Jobs

Local | World | Health ➤ Crime | Education

Let the Punishment Fit the Crime

1 In medieval times, people accused of a minor crime such as theft, trespassing or even drunkenness were often locked in a wooden frame called "stocks" in the town square. Passersby could throw garbage and rotten food at them while they served their sentence. The aim of the punishment was to cause public humiliation and warn other people that crime doesn't pay.

2 But this kind of punishment disappeared with the Middle Ages, didn't it? Not so. It would seem that "shame punishments" are making a comeback in some parts of the USA. If you had driven through Charlottesville, Virginia last week, you would have seen a strange sight. A young man dressed as the character Bert from children's show *Sesame Street* was standing outside a store holding up a sign. It wasn't an ad but a form of punishment—for a teenage shoplifter.

3 Store owner Andrew Perry caught the 18-year-old stealing from his store and offered him a choice: either he called the police or the boy could stand outside the store for two days holding a sign saying "I got caught shoplifting at Halloween Express." Mr. Perry says that he was trying to be generous. If he had reported the crime, the boy would have ended up with a criminal record, which could have affected him for the rest of his life. No one wants to employ someone with a criminal record.

4 This is one of many recent cases of offenders being given the choice between a short-term prison sentence or carrying a sign advertising their crime. But is this any different from putting people in stocks? It seems distasteful in this day and age to use public humiliation as punishment.

Done

Comments in chronological order (Total 2 comments)

Post a comment

5 We need more of this kind of thing! Public humiliation really works, as many people can't imagine anything worse. Offenders accept responsibility and think twice about committing another crime. Others are deterred from committing the same crime as they don't want to experience this embarrassment. And society is given the satisfaction of seeing that criminals are being punished. If this type of punishment were more common, we might not need so many prisons.

Spongebob | Posted 09 October 6:26 p.m.

6 Why don't we go one step further and bring back the stocks? Public humiliation is an attack on human dignity. And it is counterproductive—it wouldn't reduce crime if we used this form of punishment more. On the contrary, it would trigger anger and antisocial behavior. It would just be a form of entertainment for the masses and could even encourage mob justice.

DustyDan | Posted 10 October 10:04 a.m.

Grammar

1 a Choose the correct options to complete the extracts.

a It *would / wouldn't* reduce crime if we used this type of punishment more.

b If this type of punishment were more common, we *might / might not* need so many prisons.

c If he had reported the crime, the boy *would / wouldn't* have ended up with a criminal record, which *could / couldn't* have affected him for the rest of his life.

b Check your answers in the text in SPEAKING & READING.

2 a Look at the sentences in 1a and answer the questions.

1 Which sentences talk about a) the present or the future? b) the past?

2 Are the situations real or imagined?

3 Look at the verbs in italics. Which describe a) a definite consequence? b) a possible consequence?

b Underline the verbs that follow *if* in 1a. Then complete 1–8 in the GRAMMAR PANEL with the words in the box.

could have + past participle infinitive future *might* past present *would*

3 a Rewrite sentences 1–4 so the meaning is the same. Use *might/could* where appropriate.

1 I don't use the subway after 10 p.m. because it's too dangerous.

I would .... *if it wasn't* ....

2 I left my laptop in the car and someone broke into the car and stole it.

If I .... *, the thief* ....

3 I got a parking ticket because I stayed five minutes longer than I paid for.

If I .... *five minutes earlier, I* ....

4 There's a lot of crime in my neighborhood because unemployment is high.

There .... *so much crime in my neighborhood if* ....

b Are any of the sentences in 3a true for you or the area where you live?

4 a Complete sentences 1–4 so they are true for you.

1 If I had more... I would...

2 If I ever..., the first person I would tell is...

3 If I hadn't..., I might not have...

4 I might not have... if... hadn't helped me.

b Compare your answers with a partner's. Ask follow-up questions to find out more information.

If sentences: imagined situations (1)

We can use *if* + past simple or past perfect to describe imagined situations.

a) Use *if* + past simple to describe situations in the (1) .... or (2) ....

If we used this punishment more frequently... (but we don't)

b) Use *if* + past perfect to describe situations in the (3) ....

If he had reported the boy to the police... (but he didn't)

NOTE: Some people prefer to use *were* instead of *was* with *I/he/she/it* to describe an imagined situation in the present or future. *Were* is more formal than *was*:

If he were older, he would get a prison sentence.

Describing imagined consequences

To describe the consequence of the imagined situation, we use the modal verbs *would, could* or *might*.

a) To talk about an imagined consequence in the present or future, we use *would/could*, etc., + (4) ....

b) To talk about an imagined consequence in the past, we use *would/could*, etc., + (5) ....

Would, could or *might*?

We use (6) .... to say that this is the definite consequence of the imagined situation.

We use (7) .... or (8) .... to say that the consequence is possible, but not definite:

He would have ended up with a criminal record, which could have affected him for the rest of his life.

See page 147 for grammar reference and more practice.

Speaking

1 a Work in groups of four. Turn to page 159. Read about the crimes and rank them 1–4 in order of how serious you think they are (1 = the most serious, 4 = the least serious).

b Imagine you are judges. Discuss the crimes and choose an appropriate punishment. Choose a different punishment for each crime.

2 Share your ideas with the class. Which punishment is the most common/unusual/severe?

a

b

LISTENING & VOCABULARY: Scams

1 a Work in pairs. Read the definition. The people in the images are about to become victims of a scam. What kind of scam do you think is going to take place?

> **scam** *(n)* a dishonest way to obtain money from people by tricking or deceiving them, for example, using a false identity (see also **confidence trick**)

b 8.2 Listen and check your ideas. What happened in each situation? What was stolen?

2 Listen again. Why were the scams so successful? Mark the correct options a–c for each person.

Nicky
a The person who approached her was a friend. ....
b The person only took $10. ....
c The person pretended to help her. ....

Andy
a He had lost his passport. ....
b The people were wearing uniforms. ....
c The people showed false ID cards. ....

3 a Complete the extracts with the words in the box.

argue camera city passport police situation uniform

1 Almost everyone will have been **taken in** by a scam of some kind at some time, especially if we live in, or travel to, a big ....
2 While you're trying to make sense of the .... , you don't notice what the **thief** is doing.
3 They grabbed my wallet and .... and my wife's .... and ran off. I can't believe how **naive** we were!
4 Well, the **bogus** tourist .... trick is very common.
5 You'd be amazed what most **law-abiding** citizens will hand over to a person in .... !
6 I don't think I'd .... with an **authority figure** either!

b Match the words in bold in 3a to definitions a–f.

a a person in a position of power, such as a police officer or government official
b showing lack of experience, childlike
c someone who steals something
d following society's rules
e fake, not genuine
f tricked

4 a Complete the text with the words in bold in 3a.

> We're often very (1)........................ and complain that "they didn't look like criminals" after being (2)........................ by a scam. Most (3)........................ members of society usually trust an (4)........................ and are easily tricked by a (5)........................ who pretends to be a lawyer, banker or other official. If you are not sure if someone is genuine, always ask for ID. If they can't produce proof of identity, you can be pretty sure they're (6)........................ .

b Work in pairs. Answer the questions.

- Do you think you would have been taken in by the scams described by Nicky and Andy? Why/Why not?
- Do you know of any other scams or confidence tricks? Tell the class.

Grammar

1 **a** What is the difference in meaning between a and b in sentences 1 and 2?

1 a If only I **covered** my PIN number, but I never remember to do that.
  b If only I**'d covered** my PIN number, but I forgot.
2 a I wish there **had been** some real police officers around to stop them.
  b I wish there **were** more police officers around here.

b What are the verb forms in bold in 1a? Do they refer to the past or present?

2 Choose the correct option or complete 1–6 in the Grammar Panel.

3 Complete sentences 1–6 with an appropriate form of the verbs in parentheses.

1 I wish I .... *(can)* dance, but I have two left feet!
2 If only there .... *(not be)* so many dishonest people in the world.
3 If only I .... *(learn)* another language when I was a child, I'd be bilingual now.
4 My parents wish they .... *(live)* in a country with a better climate—they hate the cold.
5 Pierre wishes he .... *(not drop out)* of college before graduating.
6 I wish I .... *(not work)* from home every day. I get really lonely.

4 **a** Make a list of five regrets about your present and past.

I didn't learn to speak Japanese when I lived in Japan.

b Work in groups. Discuss your regrets and say why you wish things were different.

I wish I could speak some Japanese. I'm sure it would help me find a job.

Wishes & Regrets

I wish.../If only...

We use *I wish/If only* + the past simple to talk about a [(1)] present / past situation that we want to be different:

Nicky doesn't cover her PIN number.

She says: If only I [(2)] .... my PIN number.

A present fact with *can/can't* changes to [(3)] could(n't) / would(n't) when we want things to be different:

Nicky can't turn back the clock.

She says: I wish I [(4)] .... turn back the clock.

We use *I wish/If only* + the past perfect to talk about wishes and regrets about [(5)] present / past situations:

Andy didn't leave his valuables in the hotel safe.

He says: If only I [(6)] .... my valuables in the hotel safe.

See page 147 for grammar reference and more practice.

Pronunciation: *Wish & if only*

1 **a** 8.3 Listen to sentences 1–4. Underline the words that are stressed most.

1 I wish the world were a safer place.
2 He really wishes he had listened to your advice.
3 If only I could help you.
4 Sam wishes she hadn't told him the truth now.

b Listen again. Why are these words stressed?

2 Work in pairs. Practice saying the sentences in 1.

Speaking

1 **a** Work in pairs. Imagine you have both been the victims of a scam. Student A, turn to page 159. Student B, turn to page 161. Then act out two conversations.

Student A

Tell your partner about the scam. Where were you? What happened? How did you feel afterward?

Student B

Listen to your partner talking about a scam. Do you think he/she was naive, or was the scam very clever? Respond to what your partner says.

b Switch roles and act out the other conversation.

2 Decide which scam was the worst. Share your ideas with the class. How many people agree with you?

Notice *grab*

The verb *grab* means "to take something very quickly with your hand":

As soon as we opened our bags, they grabbed my wallet.

We also use *grab* to mean "to get something quickly":

Is the meeting starting now? I'll just grab a cup of coffee and join you there.

■ PRACTICE *IF* SENTENCES WITH MIXED TIME FRAMES
■ TALK ABOUT PAST DECISIONS

VOCABULARY: On trial

1 a Work in pairs. Look at the images. What do they show? Who are the people? What are their roles?

b Read the information about courtrooms. Check your answers in 1a. Then put the words in bold in the correct column.

Article | Discussion

Trial

A trial normally takes place in a **courtroom**. A criminal is considered innocent until **proven guilty,** so during the trial, this person is called the **defendant**. The lawyer and legal advisers who represent him/her are called **the defense**. The defendant **pleads guilty** or **not guilty**. The lawyers who accuse the defendant are **the prosecution**. Both sets of lawyers interview **witnesses**—people who saw the crime or have specialized information. The defendant and witnesses **give evidence**. A **jury** of 12 members of the public decides if the defendant is innocent or guilty. A **judge** oversees the trial. When the jury **delivers a verdict**, the judge **passes sentence**—he/she decides whether the defendant goes to prison, pays a fine, does community service or goes free.

Places	People	Actions

a

b

2 Work in pairs. Discuss the questions.

- Is the information in the text in 1b the same in your country? If it's different, explain how.
- Do you enjoy watching courtroom dramas? Why/Why not? Do you think they give a realistic picture of real-life courtrooms?

LISTENING

1 a 8.4 Listen to the story of a real-life courtroom drama. What is the link to the image on the left? Answer the questions.

1 Who is the defendant?
2 Is he guilty?
3 What do you think will happen to him?

b Listen again. Number events a–h in the order they happened, 1–8.

a .... Marvin's mother called the police.
b .... Marvin's favorite teacher left his job.
c .... Marvin started spraying graffiti.
d .... He vandalized the railroad track.
e .... He said he was guilty.
f .... He became friendly with the wrong crowd.
g .... His grandmother lied to protect him.
h .... Marvin's mother read his text messages.

2 a Work in pairs. Answer the questions.

1 What kind of relationship did Marvin have with his mother? How do you know?
2 How did his mother know he was vandalizing the railroad tracks?
3 What evidence was there to connect Marvin to the crime?
4 Why didn't the police believe his grandmother?
5 Do we know the result of the trial? Why/Why not?

b Check your answers in Transcript 8.4 on page 164.

3 a Work in groups. What do you think of the actions of these people?

- Marvin
- his friends
- his mother
- his grandmother

b What punishment (if any) do you think Marvin should receive for his crime?

Grammar

1 a Match the sentence halves from the audio.

1 If Mrs. Duthie hadn't contacted the police,
2 If Marvin and his friends had stuck to graffiti,
3 If it wasn't so common for family members to lie to protect each other,

a the police might have believed her.
b things might not have turned out so badly.
c Marvin wouldn't be on trial here today.

b Answer the questions in pairs. Then complete 1–4 in the GRAMMAR PANEL.

1 Look at sentence parts 1–3 in **1a**. Which describe a) an imagined situation in the present? b) an imagined situation in the past? What verb forms are used?
2 Look at sentence parts a–c in **1a**. Which describe a) an imagined consequence in the present? b) an imagined consequence in the past? What verb forms are used?

2 Complete sentences 1–5 with the correct form of the verbs in parentheses. Use *could/might* where appropriate.

1 If Marvin had more respect for his mother, he .... *(not get)* into trouble with the police.
2 I would have gone to the party last night if I .... *(not have)* so much work at the moment.
3 If I spoke Spanish, I .... *(help)* you translate that letter yesterday.
4 If we hadn't missed the bus, we .... *(be)* there by now.
5 I wouldn't feel so upset if they .... *(destroy)* my favorite painting when they broke in last night.

3 a Write notes on how your life would be different if...

- the Internet hadn't been invented
- you didn't speak English
- you lived in a different country.

b Work in groups. Compare your ideas. Share the most interesting ideas with the class.

If Sentences: Imagined Situations (2), Mixed Time Frames

If sentences can contain more than one time frame.

Past & Present

An imagined situation in the past can have an imagined consequence in the present:

(1) ....

Present & Past

An imagined situation in the present can have an imagined consequence in the past:

(2) ....

Notice the verb forms that we use:

Imagined situation in the present: past simple

Imagined situation in the past: (3) ....

Imagined consequence in the present: *would/could/might* + infinitive

Imagined consequence in the past: *would/could/might* + *have* + (4) ....

See page 147 for grammar reference and more practice.

Speaking

1 a Think of a situation where you made a major decision. Answer the questions.

1 What was the decision?
2 Why did you have to make it?
3 Who was involved?
4 What happened?
5 How did you feel?
6 How did your life change afterward?

b Work in groups. Explain your decisions. Then discuss the questions.

- Do you think it was it a good decision?
- How would your life be different if you had made a different decision?

TUNE IN

1 **a** Work in pairs. Look at the images. What is happening in each one? Have you, or has anyone you know, experienced any of these things? If so, what happened?

b 8.5 Listen and match conversations 1–3 to images a–c.

a

b

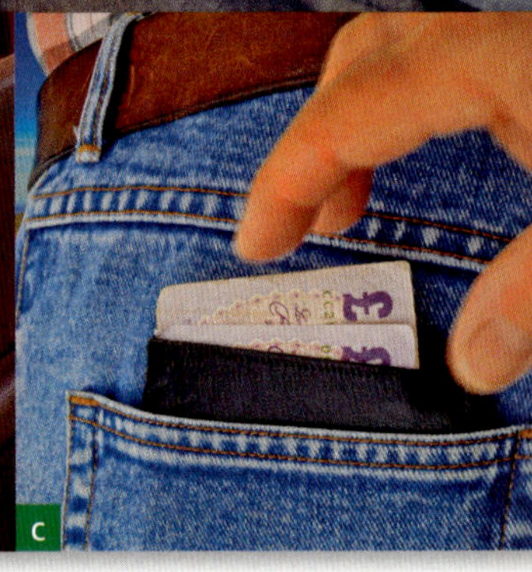
c

2 Listen again. How many different topics are there in each conversation?

3 **a** Match topics a–j to conversations 1–3.

a a TV show ...*3*... ☐
b a crime at a soccer game .... ☐
c a new model of phone .... ☐
d a car crime .... ☐
e writing a report .... ☐
f a meeting .... ☐
g the weekend *1*
h ID cards and office security .... ☐
i a crime in the office .... ☐
j borrowing something .... ☐

b Listen again and check. Number the topics in the order they are mentioned.

FOCUS ON LANGUAGE

4 **a** Complete the extracts from the audio.

1 **Before I** ...., have you e-mailed Shane about the finance meeting?
2 **By the** ...., have you heard about the new ID cards we're getting?
3 .... **about** security, did you hear that Anita had her iPhone stolen yesterday?
4 **That** .... **me**, have you seen the new Blackberry touchscreen phone?
5 .... **the subject**, did you hear about Marcela's car?
6 ...., she borrowed my GPS the other day.
7 .... **then**, I have to catch the bus in five minutes.

b 8.6 Listen and check. Why do the speakers use these expressions?

“Changing topic”

Listen again to sentences 1–7 in 4a. Underline the main stress in the expressions for changing the subject.

1 *Before I forget...*

Listen again and repeat with the correct stress.

OVER TO YOU

5 **a** Choose five different topics from the box. Prepare notes on what you could say about each topic.

- a trip you've just returned from
- a trip you're going on soon
- good news at work
- good news about your family
- a movie you've seen recently
- a book you're reading
- some music you bought last week
- a concert you went to
- the weather
- gossip about a mutual friend
- some local news
- an important sporting event

b Work in pairs. Act out a conversation about several topics. Continue until you have talked about all your topics.

Student A

Start a conversation with your first topic.

Student B

Discuss the topic with your partner. Then change the subject and talk about one of your topics, etc.

TUNE IN

1 Look at the image and read the blog post. What happened exactly?

Status update | View all comments (1) | Go to latest comment

I've invested months of time in the virtual world NewUniverse. Yesterday a gang of animated characters invaded my virtual home and stole all my virtual belongings, which took me months of work and a lot of money to obtain. These things can now be sold to other people. Isn't it time the police were called in to investigate this kind of crime?

posted by Francesca at 20:36

2 Read Margarita's reply to the blog post. Are sentences 1–4 true or false according to her reply?

1 Margarita can't understand why Francesca is upset.
2 Virtual property should be treated the same as property in the real world.
3 Psychologists say that virtual crime does not affect victims as much as real-life crime.
4 Real people don't commit a crime, only their avatars.

Comments | View status update

I'm really sorry to hear about this, Francesca! I couldn't agree with you more! You've invested time, emotion and real money in your virtual home and belongings, so I'm not surprised you're upset. There's now a full range of crimes taking place in virtual worlds, and the consequences can be very real. In fact, psychologists have found that for people who invest hours a day in their online characters, these crimes can be just as difficult to deal with as the real-world version.

And, of course, virtual items often have a real-world value. Criminals can make thousands of dollars by stealing online identities and belongings, and then selling them to other people. There's no question that virtual property should enjoy the same protection as tangible property! In addition, the people who create avatars to commit these crimes have stolen users' passwords to access their accounts. So there are actually two crimes being committed here! I strongly believe that these criminals need to be punished.

posted by Margarita at 22:47

3 Work in groups. Discuss the questions.

- Do you disagree with any of Margarita's arguments? Which ones? Why?
- What do you think should be the penalty for crimes like this?

PREPARE FOR TASK

4 Find phrases in Margarita's reply that...

1 express agreement. *(1 phrase)*
2 express absolute certainty. *(2 phrases)*
3 add an extra point to an argument. *(1 phrase)*
4 refer to official research. *(1 phrase)*

5 Work in pairs. Choose one of the posted comments. Do you agree with it? Prepare notes on why/why not.

Comments | View status update

We need CCTV cameras everywhere. They're a very successful crime deterrent. Preventing crime and catching criminals is all that matters.

File sharing is not a crime. People just want to share and experience more, and now we have the technology to do this.

TASK

6 Write a blog post reply giving your opinion on the comment you chose in 5. Use the reply in 2 as a model. Include some expressions from 4.

REPORT BACK

7 Read each other's replies. Did anyone have similar arguments? Who had the most convincing arguments?

➜ Go to Review C, Unit 8, p. 103

9 LUCK AND FORTUNE

a

b

d

c

e

f

g

1 Look at the images. They show lucky charms from around the world. What countries do you think they come from?

2 a Work in groups of three. Student A, turn to page 159–161. Student B, turn to page 159. Student C, turn to page 160. Read about the lucky symbols. Complete the chart for your symbols.

Image	Name	Country/ Countries	Meaning or origin	Where you find it/ Use
a				*temples – rub heads for luck*
b	*terracotta bulls*			
d				*entrance to house/business*
e			*protect you from bad energy*	
f		*worldwide*		
g		*Germany*		

b Exchange information about your symbols to complete the rest of the chart. What lucky charms are common in your country?

h

3 Work in pairs. Complete A in the KEY VOCABULARY PANEL.

1

"The difference between ………… and ………… is doing a thing nearly right and doing a thing exactly right."
(Edward Simmons)

2

"We create our ………… every day—most of the ills we suffer from are directly traceable to our own behavior."
(Henry Miller)

3

"A wise man turns ………… into good …………."
(Thomas Fuller)

4

"………… in the form of ………… works exactly the same as everything else. You will see it coming into your life when you are unattached to needing it."
(Wayne Dyer)

5

"………… is not a matter of ………… . It is a matter of choice. It is not a thing to be waited for, it is a thing to be achieved."
(William Jennings Bryan)

KEY VOCABULARY

Luck

A Nouns related to luck

- 9.1 Try to complete the quotes in 3 with the words in the box. Use one word twice. Then listen and check.

chance	destiny	failure	fate
fortune	prosperity	success	wealth

- Answer the questions.
  1 What do the quotes in 3 mean?
  2 Do you agree with each quote? Why/Why not?

B Expressions with *luck*

- Match expressions 1–6 to meanings a–f.

1 with any luck	a unfortunately not
2 a stroke of luck	b have no more luck
3 run out of luck	c try too hard to get something and risk losing what you've achieved
4 wish me luck	d if things go well
5 push your luck	e say that you hope things go well
6 no such luck	f something fortunate and unexpected

- Do you use similar expressions in your own language?

4

a Work in pairs. Complete B in the KEY VOCABULARY PANEL. Use a dictionary to help you.

b Complete sentences 1–6 with the expressions from B.

1 I have my driving test this afternoon. *Wish me luck!*
2 A: Did you get tickets to the concert?
B: ………… . They were all sold out!
3 I was given an upgrade on my flight to Buenos Aires. That was ………… !
4 He usually wins the tennis match, but he didn't this month. I think he's ………… .
5 The interview went well, so ………… they'll offer me the job!
6 I think you should accept the offer. Don't ………… and ask for more.

5 Work in groups. Discuss the questions.

- Do you consider yourself lucky? Are some people born lucky?
- To what extent do you think we make our own luck in life?
- Do you believe that lucky charms work? Have you or has anyone you know experienced this?

■ PRACTICE CLEFT SENTENCES FOR EMPHASIS
■ TALK ABOUT WHAT MAKES YOU NERVOUS

SPEAKING

1 Work in pairs. Discuss the questions.

- Look at the images. What reasons might the people have for feeling nervous?
- Which situation would make you feel most nervous? Why?

2 **a** Match statements 1–4 to images a–d.

1 "It's hard trying to imagine what they're going to ask you." ....
2 "My mind goes blank as soon as I start reading the questions." ....
3 "I'm always worried I've forgotten something important." ....
4 "Just before the performance starts, I get butterflies in my stomach." ....

b Have you been in one of these situations recently? How did you feel?

LISTENING

1 9.2 Listen to a radio program about lucky rituals. Number the images in the order the situations are mentioned.

2 **a** Listen again. Take notes on each part of the program.

Part 1
1 What is a lucky ritual?
2 Why do we develop lucky rituals?
3 How can they help us?

Part 2
4 What ritual(s) does Teresa mention for each situation?

Traveling	
Job interviews	
Exams	
Performing on stage	

Part 3
5 How does Teresa believe lucky rituals work?

b Compare your notes with a partner's. Listen again to check or add information.

3 Work in groups. Discuss the questions.

- Which of the rituals in the audio do you think is the strangest? Why?
- Has a lucky ritual ever helped you or anyone you know? How did it help?

a

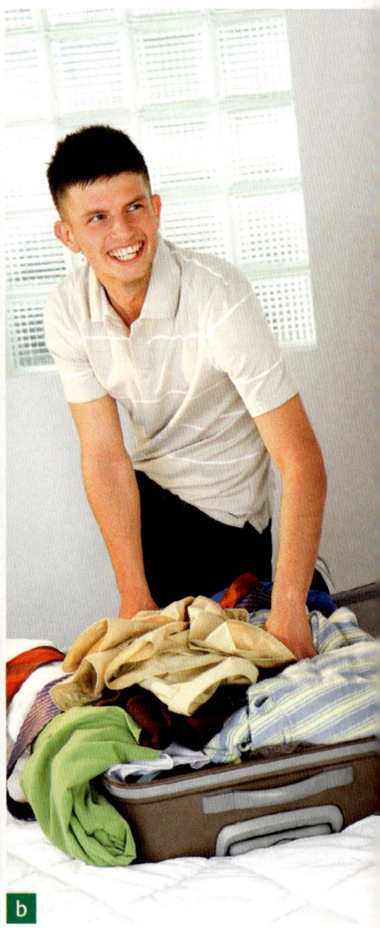
b

GRAMMAR

1 9.3 Look at the pairs of sentences. Which sentence in each pair was used in the radio program? Listen and check.

1 a Fear of the unknown makes us develop lucky rituals.
  b **It's** fear of the unknown **that** makes us develop lucky rituals.
2 a Performing on stage causes me the most anxiety.
  b **What** causes me the most anxiety **is** performing on stage.
3 a Exams cause the greatest stress.
  b **The thing that** causes the greatest stress **is** exams.
4 a Job interviews also stress people out.
  b **Another situation that** stresses people out **is** a job interview.

2 **a** Look at the pairs of sentences in 1. Underline the main topic in each sentence.

b Notice the position of the main topic in the b sentences in 1. Which word comes directly before the main topic? Complete a–d in the GRAMMAR PANEL with sentences 1b–4b.

3 **a** Put the words in order to make cleft sentences.

1 the most / speaking in public / is / anxious / what / makes me
2 prepares you / not / that / exams / for / it's / lucky rituals / studying
3 interviews / about / hate / is / I / what / unexpected questions / most
4 is / most / the / I / Judi Dench / admire / stage actor / who
5 stressed / why / the / I'm / can't / reason / I / is / that / at work / smoke

c

d

Adding Emphasis: Cleft Sentences with *Is*

We use cleft sentences to emphasize the topic of a sentence. The normal word order in the sentence changes.

We can form cleft sentences using:

1 *It's... that...*

Use *it's* to introduce the main topic. Add information about the topic after *that*:

(a) ....

2 *The thing that / The reason why... is...*

The main topic comes at the end of the sentence. We use *is* to introduce the main topic:

(b) ....

We can also use other words instead of *thing*, e.g., *situation, place, person*:

(c) ....

3 *What... is...*

The main topic comes at the end of the sentence. Use *is* to introduce the main topic:

(d) ....

See page 148 for grammar reference and more practice.

b Do you agree with sentences 1–5 in 3a? If not, change them so they are true for you. Compare your sentences with a partner's.

4 Complete the conversation using cleft sentences with the words in parentheses.

A Are you ready for your trip to Asia? I bet you're looking forward to visiting all those countries!

B Actually, (1) what... *(lying on a beach)*

A But it'll be great to visit Thailand!

B Well, (2) the place I really want... *(Vietnam)*

A Are you nervous about the flight? I know flying makes you anxious!

B Not really. (3) It's only... *(turbulence)*

A And crowded airports are stressful.

B I know, but (4) what I find... *(going through security)*

A I suppose it'll be challenging using local transportation.

B Yes, but (5) it's... *(trying to speak the local languages)*

5 a Work in pairs. Rewrite the conversation in 4 about another situation, e.g., a job interview or exam.

b Act out your conversations with a partner from another pair.

Notice *What I really...*

We often use *really* + a state verb (e.g., *like, love, hate, enjoy, want, need*) with *What* clauses in cleft sentences:

What I really love is exploring new places.
What I really need is a good night's sleep.

Speaking

1 a Work in pairs. Make a list of other situations that commonly cause anxiety.

b Choose one situation from 1a or images a–d. Write notes on how you can prepare for the situation in order to reduce anxiety.

What I find helpful before an interview is...

2 Work with a pair who chose a different situation. Listen to their advice. Do you think they gave good advice? Why/Why not?

SPEAKING & VOCABULARY: Sports

1 Work in pairs. Discuss the questions.

- Who is the greatest athlete in your country?
- Why do you think he/she is so successful?

2 **a** Match the words in the box to images a–e. Use a dictionary to help you. Which four items are *not* shown in the images?

> bat cap club course court field goggles helmet knee pads racket skates stadium track

b Put the words in 2a in the correct column. Then add three more words to each column.

Equipment	Places
bat	

3 **a** Work in pairs. Match sports to some of the words in 2a to make collocations.

baseball bat *swimming/baseball cap*

b What sports do you play? What equipment do you use?

READING

1 Read the article. Which athletes...

1 are successful due to a physical advantage over competitors according to the media?
2 are successful due to the amount of practice they put in according to the writer?

2 Correct these false statements.

1 Journalists claim that Phelps is faster than other swimmers because he has longer legs.
2 In the past, successful sprinters were usually tall.
3 Natural ability is the most important quality for a successful athlete.
4 Ochoa's success was due mainly to talent.
5 Successful athletes only need to train physically to perform at their best.

3 Find words in the article that mean...

1 having unusually flexible joints *(adj) (para. 1)*.
2 the processes and functions of an organism *(n) (para. 1)*.
3 having a short, solid build *(adj) (para. 2)*.
4 getting more of *(v) (para. 3)*.
5 to continue trying to do something despite difficulties *(v) (para. 5)*.

4 Work in pairs. Do you agree with the article? What do you think makes a successful athlete?

"The more I practice, the luckier I get!"

1 Can we make our own luck, or are some people just born lucky? This question is particularly relevant in sports. Whenever a new star athlete appears, journalists try to explain their success by describing their physical characteristics. Swimmer Michael Phelps is a classic example. He's already the greatest swimmer in Olympic history and one of the most successful Olympians of all time. However, writers explain his abilities by saying that he is double-jointed, so he is more flexible than other swimmers; he has bigger feet to give him extra power in the water; none of his competitors have arms as long as his. Phelps's physiology seems to indicate that he was born lucky.

2 Similar explanations have been given for Jamaican sprinter Usain Bolt's success. At 1.95 meters tall, Bolt has changed the world of running. Many believe he is the finest sprinter the world has ever seen. He has broken the world record for the 100 meters three times and for the 200 meters twice. Although, historically, most successful sprinters have been short and stocky, the press has often put Bolt's success down to being a breed of superhuman giant.

3 But sports stars are made, not born. In sports, dedication is as important as natural ability. When

GRAMMAR

1 Read sentences a–c from the article. Match them to 1–3 in the GRAMMAR PANEL.

a Many believe he is the finest sprinter the world has ever seen.
b The more determined and motivated you are, the more successful you will be.
c Ochoa spent hours practicing to become more and more accurate.

2 Complete the text. Use the correct form of the adjectives in parentheses where given.

Boxer **Joe Walcott** was born in British Guyana in 1873. Some experts say he was (1) .... *(great)* fighter of his weight that the boxing ring (2) .... ever known. Walcott coined the phrase, "The (3) .... *(big)* they are, (4) .... *(hard)* they fall." Despite his short stature he went on to beat (5) .... and .... *(large)* opponents, whose punches usually landed on his shoulders. Between 1901 and 1904 he became (6) .... and .... *(powerful)*, until he accidentally shot himself in the hand. (7) .... *(weak)* his hand got, the (8) .... *(successful)* he became, until he finally retired from boxing in 1911.

people praised golfer Gary Player's luck, he said, "The more I practice, the luckier I get." This is very true. Along with a commitment to hard work, the more determined and motivated you are, the more successful you will be. Bolt does three hours of intensive training every day. It's also a lesson well learned by Mexican golfer Lorena Ochoa, who is one of the most successful female golfers ever. While piling up trophies, Ochoa spent hours practicing to become more and more accurate. Discipline and structure were the key to her success. The style, flair and creativity she showed on the course were a direct result of her strict adherence to a training and practice regime.

4 In addition, athletes repeatedly visualize themselves being successful in order to get into the right frame of mind. Mental preparation is essential for producing maximum performance.

5 All these athletes have risen above the crowd simply because their teammates are less dedicated than they are. No one comes into the world able to use a baseball bat or kick a football or soccer ball. The true secret to being lucky is to see yourself as you would like to be, to visualize the result you really want and to work hard and persevere until you achieve it.

3 a Complete the sentences so they are true for you.

1 ... is the ... athlete I've ever watched. He/She gets ...er and ...er every year.
2 ... is becoming more and more ... all over the world.
3 The older I get, the less ... I become.
4 Whenever I think of ..., I get ...er and ...er.
5 The farthest I've ever ... is ...

b Compare your answers in groups. Ask follow-up questions to find out more information.

MAKING COMPARISONS

Comparatives with *and*

We link two comparatives with *and* to show that something becomes progressively greater in quality or quantity:

(1) ....

We use *more and more... / less and less...* or *-(i)er and -(i)er*:

more and more difficult / less and less energetic / happier and happier

Comparatives with *the... the...*

We use *the* + two comparatives with *more/less* or *-(i)er* to show that the second part of the sentence is the result of the first:

(2) ....

Superlative + present perfect

We use the superlative + present perfect to compare a person/event to our experience up to now:

(3) ....

See page 148 for grammar reference and more practice.

SPEAKING

1 a Work in pairs. Choose an outstanding athlete. Write notes under these headings. Use the article to help you.

Name, age, nationality, sport
Achievements
Physical characteristics
Mental characteristics

b Work with a different partner. Discuss your athletes. Compare their achievements and characteristics.

2 Report back to the class. Which athlete is the most successful/ determined/powerful? Why?

- Practice modifying comparatives
- Talk about the television and movie industry

a

b

Speaking & Listening

1 **a** Work in pairs. What jobs are the people in the images doing?

b How would you usually get each job? What qualities do you need to do each one?

2 9.4 Read the summary. Then listen to a podcast. What is the link between images a–b and the podcast?

Today we discuss working in the television and movie industry. Most people think this profession is impossible to get into unless you have the right family or connections. "Good luck with that," your friends say with a smirk when you tell them of your intentions. "It's not ***what*** *you know; it's* ***who*** *you know."*

3 **a** Which two reasons for getting a job in the television and movie industry are not mentioned in the podcast?

1 knowing the right people ....
2 having relevant work experience ....
3 having a rich family ....
4 being the best candidate for the job ....
5 having the right skills and training ....
6 going to a good school ....
7 applying for hundreds of jobs ....
8 being in the right place at the right time ....

b Listen again and check.

4 Work in pairs. Take notes on what the podcast says about the reasons in 3a. Listen again to check or add information.

5 Work in groups. Do you think the reasons in the podcast apply to other industries as well? If so, which ones?

Grammar

1 **a** Read the sentences. Underline the words that modify the comparisons.

1 This month's podcast topic isn't quite as serious as the last one.
2 Living costs are far higher than in other parts of the country.
3 It's slightly easier if your parents help you.
4 Creative industries are nowhere near as open as other professions.
5 Training is just as important as contacts.
6 Bollywood isn't any less competitive than Hollywood.

b For 1–6 in 1a, do the underlined words show...

- a big difference?
- a small difference?
- no difference?

2 Complete 1–6 in the Grammar Panel with modifying words in 1a.

3 a Complete the text with the words in the box. Some can go in more than one blank.

a little bit far just much nowhere near slightly

I really enjoyed the podcast! It was (1) .... more interesting than last week's. The program was about getting into the best universities in England. Apparently, it's really hard—it's (2) .... as difficult as working in movies or TV. It's (3) .... easier to get into a top university if you go to an expensive school first. Students from state schools are (4) .... as likely to go to top universities as those from private schools. Five elite private schools send more students to Oxford and Cambridge than 2,000 other schools combined! The situation is (5) .... better than in the past, though not much. The universities now accept students from state schools who show promise in the interview, even if their grades are (6) .... lower than those of private school students.

b Work in pairs. Is the situation similar in your country? Why/Why not?

Modifying Comparisons

We modify comparative adjectives to show there is...

1 a big difference between two things. Use *much*, *a lot* or (1) .... + comparative adjective + *than*:

Tokyo is a lot more expensive than Mumbai.

Use (2) .... *near* or *not nearly* + *as* + adjective + *as*:

My university isn't nearly as exclusive as people think.

2 a small difference between two things. Use *a little bit* or (3) .... + comparative adjective:

My sister is a little shorter than me.

Use *not* (4) .... + *as* + adjective + *as*:

The exam wasn't quite as difficult as last year.

3 no difference—one thing is equal to another. Use (5) .... + *as* + adjective + *as*:

I'm just as angry about it as you are!

Use (6) .... in questions/negatives + comparative adjective:

Is the train any cheaper than flying?

See page 148 for grammar reference and more practice.

Pronunciation: Modifying comparisons

1 9.5 Listen and underline the words that are stressed most in each sentence.

1 Life is much easier if you have rich parents.
2 Living costs in capital cities are far higher than in other parts of the country.
3 The media is nowhere near as open as other professions.
4 The right training is just as important as contacts.
5 It's a little easier to get into a top university than it used to be.

2 Practice saying the sentences in **1** with the correct stress.

Vocabulary: Verb collocations

1 a Complete the sentences with the words in the box.

care low mind rid sight touch

1 **Bear in** .... that you may need to work without pay for a year or more to get work experience.
2 You could always take out a bank loan if you're **running** .... on cash.
3 If you have a relative in the industry and you want a job, they'll **take** .... **of** it for you.
4 I **lost** .... **with** him for a while, but I got an e-mail from him last week.
5 A photographer was taking pictures... when he **caught** .... **of** one of the workers.
6 She **got** .... **of** her factory job and became a very successful model.

b Check your answers in Transcript 9.4 on page 165.

2 a Replace the words in bold with the correct form of a verb collocation from **1a**.

1 Is there a school friend or family member that you **haven't spoken to for a long time** and would like to see again?
2 What should people **remember to do** when they write a CV in your country?
3 Have you ever **briefly seen** an ad that changed your life (e.g., for a job or apartment)?
4 What do you usually do if your energy is **almost used up**?
5 Have you ever **thrown** something **away** and then discovered that you needed it?
6 Who usually **organizes** paying the bills in your home?

b Work in pairs. Ask and answer the questions in 2a. Find out as much information as you can.

Speaking

1 Work in groups. Discuss how you've been lucky or unlucky in life. Do you think your successes are due to

- belief?
- hard work?
- timing?
- good fortune?
- determination?
- other reasons?

TUNE IN

1 a Work in pairs. Look at the images and discuss the questions.

- Where are the people? What's happening?
- What do you think they're arguing about?
- What kinds of things usually cause arguments a) at home? b) at work/school/college? Make a list.

b Compare your list with another pair's. How many topics do you have in common?

2 a Match sentences 1–5 to image a or b.

1 It's still not quite what we're looking for. ....
2 No wonder you lose everything! ....
3 Just because I work from home doesn't mean I watch TV all day! ....
4 We've been working to a very tight schedule. ....
5 Can I ask everyone to send their final comments by Friday? ....

b 9.6 Listen to two conversations and check your answers in 2a.

3 Listen again. Are the statements true or false? Correct the false statements.

Conversation 1

1 The woman hasn't been working in the garden recently.
2 The man is happy to do more housework because he works from home.
3 The man thinks the woman works harder than him.

Conversation 2

4 The woman isn't satisfied with the revised website.
5 She thinks there are too many photos on the site.
6 The man doesn't agree that the site should be more colorful.

FOCUS ON LANGUAGE

4 Complete the sentences with the words in the box.

case	come	exaggerate	joking
point	suppose	there	understand

1 Oh, ... on!
2 Don't .... !
3 You must be .... !
4 I .... what you're saying.
5 That may be the .... but...
6 I'm not sure I agree with you ....
7 I get your .... but...
8 I .... you're right.

5 Which expressions in 4...

1 show disagreement?
2 concede a point in an argument?
3 are appropriate for a formal situation?

Contradicting

9.7 Listen to phrases a–d.

a Oh, come on!
b Don't exaggerate!
c You must be joking!
d You can't be serious!

Answer the questions.

1 How does the speaker sound?
2 Which word in each sentence is long and drawn out? How does this affect the meaning?
3 Does the intonation go up or down at the end of the phrases?

Practice saying the phrases with the correct stress and intonation.

OVER TO YOU

6 Work in pairs. Read the role cards. Discuss what you think the two people would say to each other. Then act out the situation using appropriate phrases from 4.

Student A

You've been waiting for a friend for over half an hour. You've tried texting and phoning to find out where he/she is, but there's no answer. This isn't the first time this has happened. You're not happy!

Student B

You got held up at home when a friend called you. Then the battery in your phone ran out. You know you're late, but you don't really think it's a problem. You know your friend will wait for you, as he/she always does.

7 a Look back at the list of topics you made in 1a. Choose one of the situations and write two role cards for it.

b Exchange your role cards with another pair. Act out the new situation.

TUNE IN

1 Look at the images. What are the people doing? What are the similarities between the two situations? What are the differences?

a

b

2 a 9.8 Listen to a short talk. Who is giving the talk, the speaker in image a or b?

b Choose the best option 1–3 to reflect the speaker's opinion.

1 She doesn't believe in luck.
2 She thinks luck plays an important role in life.
3 She thinks luck exists, but other factors are more important.

3 a Listen again. Number the three main points of the talk, a–c, in the order you hear them.

Lucky people...

a learn from bad experiences. ....
b are optimists; they deal with failure until they experience success. ....
c get involved in lots of different situations to increase their opportunities. ....

b Work in pairs. What other factors do you think influence success in life?

PREPARE FOR TASK

4 Quickly read Transcript 9.8 on page 166. Choose the best option a–c to describe the style of the talk.

a informal and friendly
b semiformal and concise
c formal and complex

5 Look at the main sections of a talk a–c. Match phrases 1–8 to the sections.

a	to begin a talk and introduce the topic	........, ..., ...
b	to introduce or discuss the main points	1, ..., ..., ...
c	to end a talk	....

1 Another important point is that...
2 Let me start by saying that...
3 In this talk I'm going to argue that...
4 In conclusion,...
5 My final point is that...
6 The first of these is...
7 Today I'm going to discuss the question:...
8 It's important to remember that...

6 a Number the stages of preparing a talk a–g in a logical order.

a Practice the talk to check that it flows easily. ....
b Research your subject. ....
c Write an outline. ....
d Choose your topic. ....
e Write key points on separate cards as prompts. ....
f Choose two or three main ideas. ....
g Decide on the purpose (to inform, persuade, entertain). ....

b Compare your answers to 6a with a partner's. Were there any differences in the order you decided on?

TASK

7 a Work in pairs. Choose one of the topic questions. Prepare a short talk. Follow main sections a–c in 5 and stages a–g in 6. Use some of expressions 1–8 in 5.

Is playing the lottery a waste of money?

Do the hardest workers get the best jobs?

What is the key to a happy life?

b Work in groups. Take turns giving your talks. Take notes on the main points of each talk as you listen.

REPORT BACK

8 Discuss the questions with your group.

- What improvements would you suggest for each talk?
- Who gave the best talk? Why?

→ Go to Review C, Unit 9, p. 104 → Go to Writing Bank 5, p. 155

VOCABULARY

Rules & behavior

1 Work in pairs. How many adjectives can you think of for each negative prefix?

dis- il- im- in- ir- un-

dishonest, disrespectful...

2 **a** Add a suffix to each root word in the box to make an adjective.

care help flex fool self trust

b Compare your answers in pairs. Think of someone/something that each adjective describes.

My sister is the most trustworthy person I know—you can tell her anything.

Collective nouns

3 **a** Work in pairs. How many things can you describe with the words in the box? Make a list.

flock herd horde mob pack swarm

b Compare your list with another pair's. How many different answers did they have?

GRAMMAR

Past modals: *Should have/Could have*

1 **a** R12 Listen and answer the questions.

1 What country are the people in?
2 What's the animal on the sign?
3 What does the sign say?
4 What problems does this animal cause?

b Complete the sentences with *could(n't) have* or *should(n't) have*. Listen again and check.

1 I .... brought you here last month when the cherry trees were in bloom.
2 There were some outside our house last month. They .... attacked someone.
3 We .... avoided it. My mother .... left food out for the boar.
4 She .... done that if we lived in Kobe... because there's a law banning the feeding of wild boars.

2 Work in groups. Have you, or has anyone you know, ever been in danger from an animal? What happened/could have happened? What should/shouldn't the person have done?

Past modals: Speculation & deduction

3 **a** Work in pairs. Write three sentences about what must/might/can't have happened in each image.

There may/might have been an earthquake.

a

b

b Compare your sentences with another pair's. Who had the best ideas?

FUNCTIONAL LANGUAGE

Criticizing

1 **a** Complete the conversation with the words in the box.

supposed to any idea going on us anything

A The library's closed! It's always open at this time. What's (1) .... ?
B I'm sorry, but it'll be closed for a while.
A But why? We've been waiting ages to go in. No one's telling (2) .... !
B There's a problem with the electricity.
A So what are we (3) .... do now?
B I'm afraid you'll have to wait until the problem's straightened out.
A How long? I need to finish my final project. Do you have (4) .... how annoying this is?

b Work in pairs. Student A, you left your car in a parking lot, but now it's closed. Student B, you work at the parking lot. Act out a similar conversation to the one in 1a.

LOOKING BACK

- Which phrases from this unit do you think are most useful? Why?
- Which reading/listening text did you find most interesting? Why?
- Tell a partner five different ways to talk about past regrets, possibilities and speculations.

Vocabulary

Crime

1 Work in groups. Why do you think people commit these crimes? What other crimes can you add to the list?

- arson
- rioting
- shoplifting
- trespassing
- vandalism

2 **a** Complete the news story with one word in each blank.

James Vernon is awaiting trial after he (1) .... a bank and (2) .... *one* dollar. He committed the (3) .... last week. He (4) .... arrested a few minutes later and was charged (5) .... robbery. Mr. Vernon, 59, isn't too unhappy, though. He is very sick, but he's unemployed and has no medical insurance. In the USA, that means he can't be treated in a hospital. However, prisoners get free health care, so if he is found (6) .... and given a prison (7) .... , he can get the medicine that he desperately needs.

b R13 Listen and check. What do you think of James Vernon's actions?

On trial

3 Work in pairs. Explain the role of these people in a courtroom.

- defendant
- defense
- judge
- jury
- prosecution
- witness

The defendant is the person on trial...

4 **a** Complete the questions with the correct form of an appropriate verb.

1 Do you think he'll .... guilty or not guilty? Why?
2 What verdict do you think the jury will .... ?
3 What sentence do you think the judge will .... ?

b Work in pairs. Answer the questions about James Vernon in 2a.

Grammar

If sentences: Imagined situations (1)

1 Complete the sentences so they are true for you. Then compare them with a partner's.

1 If I could live anywhere in the world, ...
2 If I didn't have to work/study, ...
3 If I'd lived 100 years ago, ...
4 If I'd received better advice when I was younger, ...

b Add two more sentences about yourself using *if* + past simple or past perfect.

Wishes & regrets

2 **a** Order the words to make sentences.

1 him / only / if / that / sent / I / hadn't / text message
2 late / only / show up / if / didn't / all the time / Josh
3 never / wish / I / come / here / we / had
4 names / I / remember / could / wish / more easily / I

b Work in pairs. Have you ever felt like the speakers in sentences 1–4? Tell your partner about it.

If sentences: Imagined situations (2)

3 **a** Complete the sentences so they are true for you.

1 I'd be happier now if I had/hadn't...
2 If I could..., I might have been...
3 If I'd learned..., I might... now.
4 I would... really well now if I had/hadn't...

b Compare sentences with a partner's. Report his/her most interesting sentence to the class.

Functional Language

Changing the subject

1 **a** Complete the conversations with the phrases in the box.

by the way	speaking of exercise
that reminds me	changing the subject

1 **A** Bye then, have a nice evening.
B Bye! Oh, ... , are you going to Kim's party on Friday?

2 **A** I bought a new suit for the interview.
B .... , I need to pick my clothes up from the dry cleaner's later.

3 **A** I can't be bothered to go to the gym this evening.
B .... , did I tell you I've taken up Pilates?

4 **A** I'd recommend it, it's the best book I've read recently.
B Great, I'll read it! .... , did you hear that Yoli's house was broken into yesterday?

b Work in pairs. Begin a conversation with "What are you doing after class?" How many times can you change the subject using the phrases in 1a?

Looking Back

- What was the most surprising thing that you learned in this unit?
- Which listening activity did you find most difficult? Why?
- Use the images in the unit to remember as many words and phrases as you can in five minutes.

VOCABULARY

Luck

1 Complete the conversations with the words in the box.

any such stroke wish

1 A I got the last two seats to see the movie!
B That was a .... of luck.

2 A What time does your meeting finish?
B With .... luck it'll be finished by five.

3 A When's your interview?
B Tomorrow afternoon. .... me luck!

4 A You didn't go to the party?
B No .... luck—only Anna and Michaela were invited.

2 **a** Work in pairs. Choose two expressions with *luck* from **1**. Write two short conversations that end with these expressions.

b Work with a different partner. Read the first lines of your conversations from **2a**. Your partner guesses the second line.

Sports

3 **a** R14 Label the sports equipment in the images. Then listen and check.

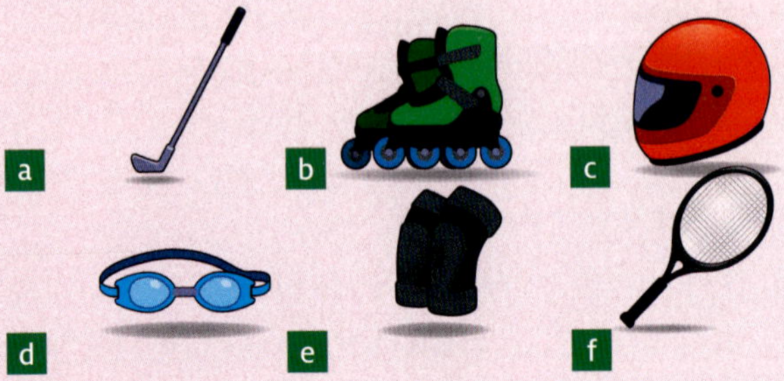

b Work in pairs. Where would you use each object in **3a** and for which sport(s)?

a golf club: on a golf course

GRAMMAR

Cleft sentences with *is*

1 **a** Circle an option and complete the sentences so they are true for you.

1 What I *love* / *hate* most...
2 A place that I really *like* / *don't like*...
3 The situation that makes me most *nervous* / *excited*...
4 It's... that really *annoys* / *bores* me...

b Work in pairs. Tell your partner about the things in **1a**. Do you have anything in common?

Making & modifying comparisons

2 **a** R15 Listen to three people arguing about sports. Which three sports do they talk about? Take notes on a) the good points and b) the bad points of each one.

b Complete the sentences. Then listen again and check.

1 Soccer isn't .... as exciting .... a good ....
2 Rugby's not .... as .... as soccer.
3 Soccer's .... as physically demanding.
4 Soccer players are .... as .... as rugby players, if not more so.
5 Basically, ... you are, ... you play...

3 Work in pairs. Do you agree with the statements in **2b**? Why/Why not?

4 Complete the sentences with your own ideas. Then discuss them with a partner.

1 Sports celebrities are becoming ....
2 By far the most .... sport is .... because ....
3 The .... sport I've ever played is .... because ....

FUNCTIONAL LANGUAGE

Arguing & making concessions

1 **a** Look at the expressions in **4** on page 100. Read the conversation and add as many expressions as you can.

A Sorry I'm late, Natalie. I missed the bus.
B You're always late, Dan.
A *Oh, come on!* It's only 10 minutes.
B We said we'd meet at 5:00 and it's 5:30 now.
A Well, I'm not *always* late.
B We've been friends for ages, and you never arrive on time for anything.
A OK. Can I buy you coffee?
B Oh, alright then.

b Compare your conversation with a partner's. Choose the best one and act it out.

LOOKING BACK

- Which lesson did you enjoy most in this unit? Why?
- Think of five new expressions you have learned for comparing things.
- Compare your most and least favorite activities with a partner's.

LISTENING

1 Work in pairs. Ask and answer the questions about reading habits.

- Do you enjoy reading in your own language?
- What kind of materials do you normally read?
- Where and when do you read?
- Do you enjoy reading in English outside the classroom?
- Do you find it easy? Why/Why not?

2 R16 Listen to a radio interview with writer Jessica Perkin. Choose the best summary 1–3.

1 Reading can improve all your language skills.
2 Reading can help you improve your vocabulary.
3 Reading can help you communicate more accurately.

3 a Take notes on what Jessica says about...

1 why reading is a good way to improve language skills.
2 reading accessible texts.
3 dealing with difficult vocabulary.

b Compare your notes with a partner's. Then listen again to check or add information.

4 R17 Complete the extracts from the audio. Then listen and check.

1 After that, ... more I read, the .... it became.
2 This is .... as effective for improving speaking accuracy .... studying grammar is.
3 If you .... read English, you .... be able to read more than half of what's on the Internet.
4 I really want to read literature, but my English is .... good enough.
5 You probably .... started with an easier text.

SPEAKING

5 a Work in groups. Make a list of reading resources in English that are available to you.

Newspaper articles (copies of The Independent at school)

b Evaluate the texts in **5a** using these questions.

- Is the content of the texts interesting to you? Why/Why not?
- How much time would you need to read each one?
- Could you enjoy the texts without the frequent use of a dictionary?

READING

6 a Choose a text from **5a** to read this week. When you have finished, complete the chart.

Title of text	
Type of text	
Reason for choosing it	
Level of language difficulty	
Would you recommend it? Why/Why not?	

b Report back to the class. Which texts would you be most interested in reading next?

QUICK CHECK

Complete the checklist below.

Can you...	Yes, I can.	Yes, more or less.	I need to look again.
1 talk about rules and appropriate behavior?	☐	☐	☐
2 speculate about past events and possibilities?	☐	☐	☐
3 discuss different crimes and punishments?	☐	☐	☐
4 talk about imagined situations in the past, present and future?	☐	☐	☐
5 talk about wishes and regrets?	☐	☐	☐
6 discuss the influence of luck on success and achievement?	☐	☐	☐
7 compare things in different ways?	☐	☐	☐
8 make and concede points in an argument?	☐	☐	☐

Compare your answers with a partner's.

- What else do you know now after studying units 7–9?
- Do you need to look again at any of the sections?
- Do you need any extra help from your teacher?

10 Value for Money

a

b

c

1 Work in groups. Look at the images and answer the questions.

- What kinds of stores do they show?
- What kinds of stores do you visit most frequently? Why?
- Which do you enjoy visiting most? Why?

2 **a** 10.1 Listen to an interview with a retail expert. Number the images in the order they are mentioned.

b Work in pairs. Answer the questions.

1 What aspect of shopping psychology do you think each image relates to?
2 In what other ways do stores try to get us to spend money?

3 **a** Match items 1–6 to a–f according to the audio. What is the purpose of each retail trick?

1 beds	a disorderly piles
2 computer products	b aluminum tables
3 fish and meat	c purple packaging
4 men's products	d pillows and duvets
5 silk scarves	e big pine tables
6 premium brands	f back of the store

(example: 1 – d)

b Listen again and check. What information surprised you most? Why?

d

4 **a** Work in pairs. Complete A in the KEY VOCABULARY PANEL.

b Work in pairs Ask and answer the questions. Ask follow-up questions to find out more information.

1 Are you saving up for anything at the moment?
2 What advice would you give someone for cutting back on spending?
3 When was the last time you were ripped off?
4 Do you think it's a good idea to take out a personal loan to pay off a credit card debt? Why/Why not?

5 Work in pairs. Complete B in the KEY VOCABULARY PANEL. Use a dictionary to help you.

6 Work in groups. Think about your favorite store. Discuss the questions.

- Where is it? Is it easy to get to?
- What kinds of things do you buy there?
- What does it look and smell like?
- Do they play music? What kind?
- How do you feel when you're in the store?
- Do you often buy things there that you don't really need?

My favorite store is a game store. They have lots of secondhand games and you can pick up some great bargains.

KEY VOCABULARY

Shopping

A Phrasal verbs about money

- Underline the phrasal verbs in the box in Transcript 10.1 on page 166. Match the verbs to meanings 1–8.

cut back fork out ~~get by~~ pay off rip off run out (of) save up take out (a loan)

1 *get by* survive day to day, especially financially
2 .... make a financial agreement with a bank or company
3 .... accumulate money for future use
4 .... spend a lot of money on something
5 .... reduce the amount that you usually spend
6 .... charge (someone) more money for something than it is worth
7 .... use all of something and not have any left
8 .... give back all the money you owe for something

- Which verbs collocate with words a–d?

a *fork out* , ... , ... money
b .... , ... a loan
c .... a debt
d .... on spending

B Materials

- Put the words in the box in the correct category.

aluminum cardboard cotton leather nylon pine plastic silk wax

Natural fibers	.... , ... , wool
Synthetic materials	.... , ... , polyester
Wood	mahogany, ...
Metal	.... , steel
Paper products	....
Other natural products	.... , rubber, ...

- What belongings do you have that are made from the materials in the chart?

a leather jacket, a mahogany table...

Speaking & Listening

1 Work in groups. Discuss the questions.

- What products do you associate with these countries?

Argentina France Italy
Japan Kuwait South Africa

When I think of Italy, I think of fashion brands like Dolce and Gabbana.

- Which products is your country famous for? What is the most famous brand?
- Are there any products from your country that are not famous but you think should be?

2 **a** Work in pairs. Look at the images. Can you answer the questions?

1 Where and what are these places? Why were they built?
2 What connection do they show between China in the past and China today?
3 What famous inventions came from China?
4 What is China famous for producing today?

b 10.2 Listen to an interview about China's economic success. How does Christopher Yu answer questions 1–4 in 2a?

3 **a** Listen again. Are these reasons for China's economic growth true, false or not mentioned?

1 China makes high-tech products.
2 Original ideas are encouraged.
3 Employees are very productive.
4 There is collaboration with overseas companies.
5 Many tourists come to visit the Great Wall.
6 There are many globally famous Chinese brands.

b What does Christopher say about the global recognition of Chinese brands?

4 Work in groups. Do you think your country is similar to China? Why/Why not? If you are from China, do you agree with Christopher?

a

b

Grammar

1 **a** Complete the sentences. Check your answers in Transcript 10.2 on page 167.

1 I bought all of them this week, and they were all made in either .... or ....
2 Neither a .... nor a .... company could employ that many people at the same time.

b Which sentence in 1oa

a compares two things and says that something is not true in each case?
b compares two things and says that something is true in each case?

2 **a** Find one more example of each type of comparison in Transcript 10.2 on page 166. What is being compared in each sentence?

b How do you say *either... or* and *neither... nor* in your language?

3 Complete 1–3 in the Grammar panel with the words in the box.

negative positive singular

4 Insert *either... or* or *neither... nor* in an appropriate position in sentences 1–5.

1 In my country there are *neither* beaches *nor* mountains. It's flat and landlocked.
2 A lot of young people here are employed studying in college. It's a problem.
3 When they graduate, most young men have to spend a year in the army do community service.
4 There are many convention centers and reception halls in my town, so most people work in catering tourism.
5 Unfortunately, there's a swimming pool a soccer stadium in my hometown.

5 Rewrite sentences 1–5 in 4 so they are true for your town/country. Compare your sentences with a partner's.

Either... or/*Neither... nor*

We use *either... or* and *neither... nor* to compare two different items.

We use *either... or* to mean "one or the other but not both." It has a (1) .... meaning:

We can visit either Shanghai or Beijing.

Neither... nor has a (2) .... meaning. It means "not the first one and not the second one":

Neither the drugstore nor the supermarket had the medicine you wanted.

In formal English we use a (3) .... verb with *either/neither*, unless the second noun or both nouns are plural:

Neither Janna nor Harry ***is*** *going to the conference.*

NOT ~~are~~ *going...*

Neither my sister nor my parents ***know*** *about this.*

Either/neither go directly before the first of the two items being compared:

They are either ***owned by foreign companies*** *or just make parts of other products.*

See page 149 for grammar reference and more practice.

Pronunciation: *So* & *well*

1 a 10.3 Listen to the extracts. Notice the pronunciation of *well* and *so*. In which sentences are they stressed?

1 Well, they were all made in either China or Taiwan.
2 Well, for a variety of reasons.
3 Well, yes, partly, but another factor is productivity.
4 Well actually, Chinese growth isn't a purely modern phenomenon.
5 So, why is China growing so fast?
6 So why do you think that is?
7 So, it's all looking very positive for the next few decades.

b Listen again and answer the questions. In which sentences...

1 does the speaker use *well* to show that he/she is going to disagree?
2 does the speaker use *so* or *well* to introduce a summary of what has been said?
3 does the speaker use *so* to introduce a question?

2 Listen again and repeat, paying special attention to the pronunciation of *so* and *well*.

Vocabulary: Adjective order

1 a Read the rule. Match the adjectives in the box to the correct category.

Chinese	huge	new	red
rubber	shiny	square	writing

When there is more than one adjective to describe a noun, they usually follow this order:

size / age / quality / shape or design / color / origin / material / role or type / noun

Note: we rarely use more than two or three adjectives with a noun.

b Put the words in bold in the correct order. Check your answers in Transcript 10.2 on page 167.

1 a **rubber round red** ball for my dog
2 a set of **table steel shiny** knives
3 a **writing pine huge** desk
4 a **engineering Swiss leading** firm
5 that **cardboard square big** box for your computer

2 a Describe images 1–4. Use two or more adjectives for each image.

1

2

3

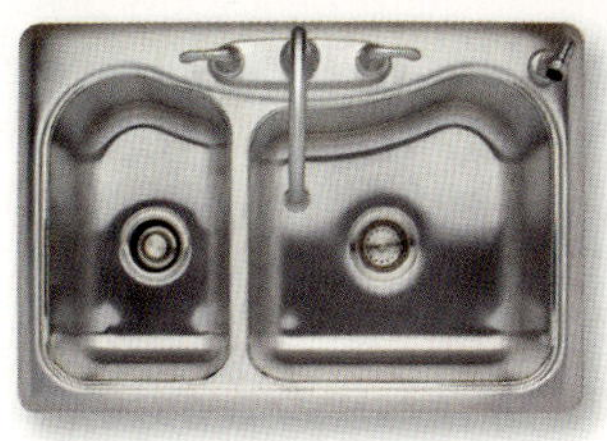

4

b Exchange sentences with a partner. Are the adjectives in the correct order?

Speaking

1 Work in groups. Think of a famous building or landmark in your country. Discuss the questions.

- Is it modern or historic? Who built it? When?
- How would you describe it?
- What is/was its purpose?
- Why is it famous? Do many people visit it?
- If you have visited it, what impression did it make on you?

2 Present your buildings or landmarks to the class. Can you add any more information to each description?

- Practice articles
- Discuss different places to shop

Susannah Clark's Blog

Shopping tips, bargain hunting, news... I am a journalist who writes about consumer issues from my base in New York.

1 How to haggle

Susannah Clark | 10:30 EST, January 9

In many parts of the world such as Latin America, Africa and Asia, haggling is expected. This is also true in street markets in southern Europe. Local markets are great places to go shopping. You can buy everything under the sun there, but there is a definite technique for haggling. If you see an item you like, don't look too interested. Decide how much it is worth to you, and then let the vendor make the first offer on the item. Make a counteroffer for half as much. Then haggle until you get to a point between the two offers you are happy with. If you are not happy with the price, try walking away. The vendor may make a better offer.

2 Buying online – a good way to shop?

Susannah Clark | 9:35 EST, January 16

Buying online is now well established and often the cheapest way of shopping. Amazon has gone from being an online bookseller to an e-commerce company and a major online provider of electronic goods, toys and games, clothes and shoes. Is it cheaper? Yes, often, but paying for shipping can also increase the cost. eBay is an online auction and shopping website, where people can buy and sell products worldwide. It can be slightly cheaper than Amazon.

3 Are garage sales a waste of time?

Susannah Clark | 11:40 EST, January 22

There are three kinds of garage or yard sale shoppers: browsers, bargain hunters and judicious shoppers. Browsers enjoy going to garage and yard sales and rarely buy anything. Bargain hunters are practical shoppers and take advantage of popular sale items like furniture and baby clothes. Judicious shoppers are the garage sale elite. They usually have a niche and are looking for pieces to fill it, whether it be antique furniture or out-of-print books. They prepare detailed lists of sites, products and prices and will search all summer for the items they collect.

4 Making the most of sales

Susannah Clark | 9:06 EST, January 29

January sales are a good time to find a bargain, but how can you make the most of this opportunity? Do some research about the items you want to buy. A bad product is a bad deal no matter how cheap it is, and some items can be a rip-off, even on sale. Decide how much money you want to spend and try not to go over the limit. It's good to compare product prices on Internet shopping sites such as PriceGrabber.com. Sites like these give good advice to bargain hunters.

Done

Reading

1 a Work in pairs. Look at the images. What do they show? What connection do they have to the lesson title?

b Match the images to blog post headings 1–4.

2 Read the four blog posts. Answer the questions in your own words. According to the blogger...

1. What's the first decision to make if you want to haggle for something?
2. Why is walking away from a vendor sometimes a good idea?
3. What are the differences between Amazon and eBay?
4. How are the three types of buyers at garage or yard sales different?
5. What are the three recommendations for finding a bargain in a sale?

3 Read the blog posts again. Find words that mean...

1. transporting goods *(blog 2)*.
2. a public sale where goods are sold to whoever offers the highest price *(blog 2)*.
3. sensible and careful *(blog 3)*.
4. specific interest or area *(blog 3)*.

4 Work in groups. Discuss the questions.

- Which of the types of shopping mentioned in the blog posts have you experienced?
- How good are you at haggling? What was the last bargain you got?
- What kinds of things do you buy online? Why? What are your favorite websites for online shopping?

NOTICE NOUNS FROM VERBS

We can make some phrasal verbs into nouns by adding a hyphen (-):

to rip off *(v) some items can be a rip-off (n) even on sale*

GRAMMAR

1 Work in pairs. Look at the words in bold in sentences a–h. Which ones have an article? Which article is used? Explain why.

- a I am **a journalist** who writes about consumer issues from my base in New York.
- b **Local markets** are great places to go shopping.
- c You can buy everything under **the sun** there.
- d If you see **an item** you like, don't look too interested.
- e Let the vendor make the first offer on **the item**.
- f **The vendor** may make a better offer.
- g Buying online is... often **the cheapest way** of shopping.
- h Judicious shoppers are **the garage sale elite**.

2 Complete 1–8 in the GRAMMAR PANEL with sentences a–h in 1.

3 a Complete the text with *a/an*, *the* or no article (Ø).

eBay is already (1) .... most successful auction site on (2) .... planet. Many of us go there to pick up (3) .... cheap gifts and (4) .... gadgets, and many people sell unusual items. But perhaps (5) .... strangest item of all was put up by (6) .... student from (7) .... Nebraska who sold (8) .... advertising space on his forehead. (9) .... space was bought by (10) .... company that makes (11) .... medicine to help you sleep. (12) .... student said, "Everywhere I went, (13) .... people wanted to talk to me. I guess that's what (14) .... advertiser wanted." Luckily (15) .... tattoo wasn't permanent. It washed off after 30 days.

b Write a short description of something you bought recently, where you bought it and what you use it for.

ARTICLES

a/an + countable noun

We use ***a*** or ***an*** to talk about...

1 jobs or professions:
(1) ....

2 something for the first time, when it has not been mentioned before:
(2) ....

the + countable or uncountable noun

We use ***the...***

3 to talk about a specific member of a group, often when it has already been mentioned:
(3) ....

4 when there is only one of something or it is obvious what we are referring to:
(4) ....

5 before a noun that is unique in the world, e.g., *the sky, the moon*:
(5) ....

6 to talk about a specific group of people:
the Japanese, the unemployed,
(6) ....

7 with ordinal numbers and superlatives: *the first offer,*
(7) ....

No article (Ø)

We don't use *a/an* or *the...*

8 when we refer to something "in general," rather than giving a specific example:
(8) ....

9 with the names of continents, regions, most countries, individual mountains and lakes:
Africa, Asia, Thailand, Mount Fuji, Lake Baikal

See page 149 for grammar reference and more practice.

SPEAKING

1 Work in groups. Decide the best place to buy these items.

1 a really rare book that is no longer on sale in bookstores
2 some unusual spices and ingredients for a dish you want to cook tomorrow
3 a computer game/cell phone that has just come on the market
4 some old clothes for a 1960s party
5 a secondhand car or motorcycle
6 some cheap furniture for your new apartment

2 Present your ideas to the class. Who had the best suggestions?

- LEARN ABOUT UNDEREMPLOYMENT
- DISCUSS JOB HUNTING

SPEAKING

1 a Read the definition. How do you think the images relate to it?

> **underemployed** *(adj)* working in a low-paid job that does not require you to use your skills and training

a

b

c

d

b Work in groups. Discuss the questions.

- Is underemployment a problem in your country?
- Who do you think it affects most? Why?
- Do you know anyone in this situation? What do they do? What are they qualified to do?

LISTENING

1 a 10.4 Listen to the first part of an interview about underemployment. Answer the questions.

1 Who does underemployment affect most?
2 Give two examples of the problems of underemployment.

b Listen again and complete the sentences.

1 Underemployment increases during...
2 If you can't get a job in your chosen industry, you may end up...
3 If you aren't using your skills, this will affect...
4 If you earn a lower salary, you won't have such a good...
5 This makes it easier to...
6 You may no longer have... or... in your job.

2 a 10.5 Listen to the second part of the interview. Which image a–d does Ryan talk about? What advice does it relate to?

b Listen again. Circle the correct option, a–c.

1 Ryan suggests additional training so that...
   a you have some qualifications.
   b you have the best skills for your industry.
   c you can get a government grant.
2 He suggests using public transportation because...
   a you may make a useful contact.
   b there are lots of job opportunities in transportation.
   c it's cheaper.
3 The first thing you need to start your own business is...
   a a boss to manage it.
   b money to invest in it.
   c to be working in a similar industry.
4 When did the flower shop start to make money?
   a After 18 months.
   b When the owner's grandmother died.
   c It never made any money.

3 Work in pairs. The interviewer asks listeners to call in with their comments. What comments would you make about...

1 the problems of low job satisfaction?
2 doing additional training to improve your skills?
3 getting money to start your own business?

VOCABULARY: Business & finance

1 Match the words in the box to definitions 1–6.

benefits	capital	expenses	grant	profit	return

1 .... the money a business makes after it pays all its costs
2 .... money given by an organization, e.g., the government, for a particular purpose
3 .... payments or advantages you get as an employee in addition to your wages
4 .... money you get back after investing in something
5 .... funds or money you use to start up a business or invest in something
6 .... the day-to-day costs of running a company

2 Work in pairs. Answer the questions. Do you know...

1 anyone who gets really good benefits in their job?
2 a company that makes a huge profit?
3 what kinds of things people receive grants for?
4 what expenses a small store usually has?
5 how to calculate how much capital you'd need to start up a business?
6 a good way to get a high return on an investment?

3 Match 1–7 to a–g to make collocations.

1 run	a debt
2 get into	b in (a business)
3 provide	c costs/the cost of
4 repay	d through college
5 cover	e a service
6 invest	f a loan
7 put yourself	g a business

4 a Complete the e-mail with the correct form of collocations 1–7 in 3.

Dear Business Guru,
I'm Ken. I'm 21, and I have money worries. I have (1) *gotten into* debt to (2) .... through college. I'm in my senior year, and I need a way to (3) .... the .... of my education and (4) .... a huge loan. I'm thinking of starting a company to design websites, but I need some capital. I think I'll be able to (5) .... an excellent ...., but I need to find people to (6) .... in my idea. Unfortunately, I don't know anything about (7) .... a business. What should I do?
Ken

b Work in pairs. What advice would you give Ken?

SPEAKING

1 a Work in pairs. Answer the questions.

1 What does the image show?
2 Who do you think made the billboard? Why?
3 Who is it aimed at?
4 Do you think it was successful? Why/Why not?

b Check your ideas on page 164.

2 a Think of a way to make a company interested in you in order to get your dream job. Think about...

- what medium you will use: poster, leaflet, networking site, etc.
- what message it will contain to get their attention
- whether it will contain an image.

b Present your ideas to the class. Which idea do you think would be most effective? Why?

a

b

c

TUNE IN

1 a Work in pairs. Where are the people in the images? How do the situations relate to the lesson title?

b Answer the questions.

- When was the last time you arranged for something to be done for you?
- What was it for? What questions did you need to ask?

2 a Work in pairs. Choose one of the images. What do you think the people are saying? Write a short conversation.

b Read your conversation out loud. Ask the class to guess the correct image.

3 a 10.6 Listen to conversations 1–3. Match them to images a–c.

b Check your answers to 1a. Did the speakers ask any of the questions from the conversations the class wrote in 2?

FOCUS ON LANGUAGE

4 a Match 1–9 to a–i to complete the sentences.

1 What's your minimum
2 Could you tell me
3 What documents
4 Will I need to pay
5 I'd like to get an estimate for
6 Do you have a budget
7 Is there a discount
8 Do you have a next-day
9 Could I arrange for

a for the job?
b delivery service?
c do I need?
d this to be delivered?
e a deposit?
f replacing the windows in my apartment.
g rental period?
h your daily rate?
i if I pay cash?

b Listen again and check. Which sentences in 4a

1 are related to money? 2 , ... , ... , ... , ...
2 ask about a service? .... , ... , ... , ...

5 What were the answers to the questions in 4a? Listen again and check.

OVER TO YOU

6 a Work in pairs. Choose a role and act out the situation.

Student A

You need to rent a minibus for a camping trip with friends. You need to know...
- the minimum rental period
- the daily rate
- if you can get an estimate
- if you need to pay a deposit
- if they offer a cash discount
- what documents you need

Call the rental company to find out the information.

Student B

You work for a car rental agency. A customer calls to find out about renting a minibus for the weekend. Answer his/her questions with the information below.

minimum rental period: *one day*
daily rate: *$230*
estimate: *$460*
deposit: *$50*
cash discount: *No. Full payment to be made by credit or debit card.*
documents: *driver's license, two utility bills for proof of address, and one other item for proof of signature*

b Switch roles and act out the situation again.

TUNE IN

1 Work in pairs. When was the last time you answered a survey? What type of survey was it? Do you like doing surveys? Why/Why not?

2 Read the survey report. Answer the questions.

1. What was the survey about?
2. What kind of people completed the survey?
3. What did people a) like? b) not like?
4. Was the survey a success? Why/Why not?

Arbon Village Store & Restaurant Survey Report

Now that many tourists are visiting Arbon Village, we decided to ask hotel guests staying in July and August about the local store and other facilities.

(1) *Here are the findings of our survey.*

(2) .... 110 people.
(3) .... (103) said that overall they were very happy with the store.
(4) .... is the proximity of the store and the fact that it provides a pleasant meeting point. This is closely followed by the excellent choice of products.

(5) .... is that prices are too high, especially for sunscreen. This is reflected by (6) .... (34) of respondents.
(7) .... , many parents are worried about protecting their children from sunburn and thought the prices were unreasonable.

There was also (8) .... (5) who would like to see extended hours in the store.

Everyone was happy with the local restaurant, (9) .... A customer complained that it had run out of fresh fish when he visited.

(10) .... (57) of our respondents said they would return next year. (11) .... was that, on average, visitors from this country spend more per day ($35) than visitors from overseas.

(12) .... , this year's survey has provided a great deal of new information about visitors to Arbon Village, and it would be useful to carry out a similar survey next year.

PREPARE FOR TASK

3 Complete the survey with phrases a–l.

- a about a third
- b Over half
- c a small number of people
- d What respondents dislike the most
- e As you might expect
- f with one exception
- g ~~Here are the findings of our survey.~~
- h In conclusion
- i One of our most interesting findings
- j The vast majority
- k We surveyed a sample of
- l What respondents like the most

4 a Work in pairs. Write eight survey questions to find out about your classmate's shopping habits. Think about…

- what stores people visit
- when/how often they shop
- what products they shop for
- how much money they spend
- how they usually pay
- if they're happy with the service they receive.

How do you usually pay when you go shopping?

I usually pay cash as I don't want to get into debt!

b Interview half the class each. Write down of the responses. Then compare your findings with your partner's.

TASK

5 Write a report of your survey findings. Use the survey report in 2 as a model. Include some of the expressions in 3.

- Write a brief introduction.
- Divide your report into paragraphs.
- Include an interesting result.
- Write a conclusion.

REPORT BACK

6 Read each other's reports. What were the most surprising results?

➔ Go to Review D, Unit 10, p. 136

11 TECHNOLOGY

1 Work in pairs. Look at the images and answer the questions.

- Where would you see each keyboard or keypad?
- Which have you used in the last 24 hours?
- Which have you never used?
- Can you think of any other examples of keyboards and keypads in everyday use?

2 a 11.1 Listen to someone talking about a new keyboard. Match it to one of the images a–f.

b Complete the notes about the keyboard. Then compare your answers with a partner's.

Name:

Main feature:

Other features:

Origin of the idea:

3 a Look at the words in bold and their definitions in A in the KEY VOCABULARY PANEL. Listen again and complete the sentences.

1 The speaker claims the fast finger keyboard is quite a **breakthrough** because...
2 The main **drawback** of early alphabetical keyboards was...
3 The inventor got her **flash of inspiration** when...
4 It has not been a **commercial success** because...
5 **Early adopters** say...
6 The speaker asks if we think this **gadget** is just another **gimmick** or...

b Work in pairs. Answer the questions.

- Do you think the keyboard is just another gimmick? Why/Why not?
- What was the last piece of new technology you bought? Why did you buy it?
- Are you usually an early adopter? Why/Why not?
- Can you think of any new technological breakthroughs in the news recently? Are they genuine breakthroughs or just gimmicks?

4 Work in pairs. Complete B and C in the KEY VOCABULARY PANEL.

5 Work in groups. Think about your first computer or cell phone. Answer the questions.

1 How was it different from the one you have today? Think about...
- size
- speed
- Internet connection
- programs (graphics, etc.)
- games.

I remember our first computer took ages to start when you turned it on.

2 Was there anything you preferred about the old model? If so, what?

KEY VOCABULARY

Talking about ideas & inventions

A Key nouns

breakthrough a discovery or a solution to a problem

commercial success something that sells a lot and makes a lot of money

drawback a disadvantage

early adopters people who buy/use new high-tech products when they first appear on the market

flash of inspiration a sudden very good idea

gadget a small mechanical or technological device or tool

gimmick something that is intended to draw attention but is not really useful

B Word building: *-al/un-*

- Add *-al* to the nouns in the box to form adjectives.

convention	inspiration	logic
nature	origin	tradition

traditional

- Which of the adjectives can you use to describe the fast finger keyboard?
- Look at the adjectives again. Which can you not add the prefix *un-* to? Which negative prefix can you add?

C Getting ideas

- Underline expressions for "getting ideas" in Transcript 11.1 on page 166. Complete 1–4 with the words in the box.

got	out	struck	up

1 It .... them that...
2 They figured .... a way to...
3 Someone came .... with the idea of...
4 The inventor .... the idea from...

- Think of a problem you had to solve recently. How did you find the solution? Use the expressions to explain the situation to a partner.

SPEAKING & READING

1 Work in groups. Look at the images of candidates for the Invention of the Year award. What do you think these inventions do?

2 **a** Work in pairs. Student A, turn to page 160. Student B, turn to page 162. Read the blog post and check your ideas in 1.

b Complete the chart for your invention.

	Engkey	Waterboxx
Inventor		
Nationality		
Purpose of invention		
Place(s) used		
Cost		

3 **a** Work in pairs. Tell your partner about your invention. Use the chart in 2b as a guide.

b Read about the other invention. Make a note of any information your partner left out.

4 Choose *Engkey*, *Waterboxx*, *Both* or *Neither* and the correct options to complete sentences 1–5.

1 .... *was / were* invented to solve an environmental problem.
2 .... *is / are* used in the countryside.
3 .... *has / have* some limitations in *its / their* use.
4 .... *was / were* designed to make people behave better.
5 .... *was / were* invented by an amateur scientist.

5 Work in groups. Which invention do you think should win the award? Why?

a

b

GRAMMAR

1 **a** Read sentences a and b. Answer the questions for each sentence.

a Engkey is the kind of teacher **who doesn't accept errors**.
b Many areas of the world receive very little rainfall, **which makes growing trees a real challenge.**

1 What do the phrases in bold describe?
2 If you take away the words in bold, does the sentence still make sense?

b Read the GRAMMAR PANEL. Which sentence in 1a has...

1 a defining relative clause?
2 a nondefining relative clause?

2 a Complete the text with relative pronouns.

It's here at last, the invention ⁽¹⁾ *that* .... everyone's been waiting for. The world's first 3D television ⁽²⁾ .... doesn't require you to wear glasses has hit the market! Toshiba, ⁽³⁾ .... has long been a leader in the home entertainment industry, has launched two models. The pictures are created with multiple lenses ⁽⁴⁾ .... direct light from the screen to points in front of the TV. The test audience at the trade show, ⁽⁵⁾ .... had originally watched *Avatar* in 3D in a movie theater, said they loved seeing it again on the new screens.

b Look again at relative clauses 1–5 in 2a. Answer the questions for each one.

1 Is it defining or nondefining?
2 Can you omit the relative pronoun?

3 a Complete sentences 1–4 so they are true for you. Add commas if necessary.

1 The most famous inventor from my country is .... who ....
2 The last electronic device I bought was a .... that ....
3 My first English teacher was .... whose lessons ....
4 On the weekend I often go to .... where ....

b Compare your answers with a partner's.

Relative Clauses

We use relative clauses to give more information about a person or object.

Defining relative clauses

In defining relative clauses...

1 the sentence is not complete, or does not make sense, without the extra information:
Engkey can only correct mistakes that are already in its database.

2 *who* can replace *that:*
He was the child who asked to be allowed in.

3 if the word *who* or *that* (the relative pronoun) is the object of the relative clause, it can be omitted:
It has a tough teaching technique (that) the students sometimes don't expect!

Nondefining relative clauses

Nondefining relative clauses

1 give additional information. The sentence still makes sense without this information:
Dr. Choi-taek is a specialist in robotics, which is increasingly important in his country.

2 give extra information on the whole sentence:
The kids think their teacher sounds rather robotic today, which is hardly surprising.

3 are separated from the rest of the sentence by a comma.

Note We don't use *that* or omit the relative pronoun in nondefining relative clauses.

See page 150 for grammar reference and more practice.

Pronunciation: Relative clauses

1 11.2 Listen to two sentences. What differences do you notice in the intonation?

1 The invention that won the award helps the environment.
2 The invention, which won the award, helps the environment.

2 a Listen again. Why does the first sentence use *that* and the second sentence use *which*?

b Practice saying the sentences with the correct intonation.

3 Practice reading the text in **Grammar 2a** with the correct intonation.

Speaking

1 a Work in pairs. What do you think has been the most important invention in the last 100 years? Why?

b Share your answer with the class. Which invention did most people choose?

LISTENING

1 **a** Work in pairs. Look at the gadgets in the images. What do you think they do?

b 11.3 Listen to a podcast about the gadgets. Number them in the order they are mentioned. Were you right about their uses?

2 Listen again. Which gadget a–f does Gabrielle recommend…

1 for someone who travels with a laptop? ....
2 as a treat for herself? ....
3 for someone who plays computer games? ....
4 for a young child? ....
5 for someone with a hand or arm injury? ....
6 for a forgetful person? ....

3 **a** Work in pairs. Complete the descriptions of the gadgets.

1 This automatic can opener can be operated using only .... hand. It opens .... and jars, as well as cans.

2 The pet drinking fountain is very simple. Just connect it to a .... supply. The simple ....-sensitive pad activates the fountain, and your pets can get themselves a drink whenever they want.

3 This great little idea not only works, it looks good as well! The WiFi logo on the front of the T-shirt .... when it approaches a WiFi hotspot. The stronger the .... , the more it lights up. Simple but very effective.

4 Computer games take on a whole new dimension with Scentsciences. Simply hook it up to your ...., and you will not only be able to see and hear your latest games, you'll be able to .... them, too!

5 This fun little gadget moves its .... in time to any sounds it picks up. Great for .... —but a hit with adults as well!

6 The 3D version of the Nintendo DS .... has been very successful, combining great 3D .... with the ability to record your own short 3D movies.

b Listen again and check.

4 Work in small groups. Discuss the questions.

- Would you buy any of these gadgets? If so, who for? If not, why not?
- When was the last time you bought a gadget? What was it? Who was it for?

a

b

c
d

e

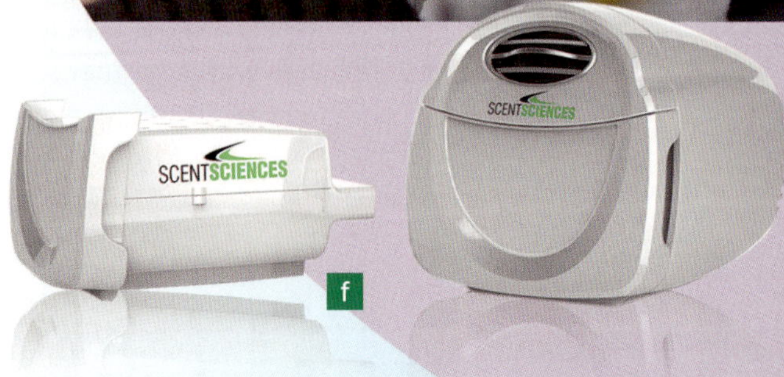

f

VOCABULARY: Describing gadgets

1 Look at sentences 1–6 from the audio. Which image a–f do they describe?

1 It has a **touch-sensitive** pad. ....
2 It's a **lightweight**, white, plastic box. ....
3 It's very cool, with a **rounded**, black, **metallic** design. ....
4 It's a **slim**, **handheld** device. ....
5 It's a little, **high-tech** box. ....
6 It was a truly **cutting-edge** piece of hardware. ....

2 **a** Work in pairs. Take turns explaining the meaning of the words in bold in 1.

b How many objects can you describe using the words in 1? Make a list.

touch-sensitive – lamp, keyboard, switch...

3 Look again at your list in 2b. Which of the objects do you have? Which would you like to have? Why?

SPEAKING & LISTENING

1 Work on your own. Make a list of all the electrical appliances and gadgets you have used in the last 24 hours. Use the images to help you.

2 **a** Work in pairs. Compare your lists. Divide the items into groups used for...

- work
- study
- fun
- household/everyday chores
- other.

b Decide which appliance or gadget is most important in each group and why.

3 **a** Compare your answers as a class. Vote on the number one most important appliance or gadget.

b 11.4 Listen to someone talking about an important gadget. Answer the questions.

1 Is it the same as the gadget you voted for in 3a?
2 Why did she give the gadget up for a week?
3 What did she miss most?
4 How did she feel about giving it up?

4 Listen again. Make a list of the things she uses the gadget for. How did living without the gadget change her life?

5 **a** Imagine you have agreed to live without your favorite appliance or gadget for a week, as part of an experiment. Discuss the questions.

- What impact would this have on your day-to-day life?
- Would any areas of your life improve? If so, which ones? How?

b Present your ideas to the class. Would most people feel better or worse? Why?

Generation Y

a

The first thing you notice when you walk into a modern classroom is the noise and energy. I've never seen such chaos! Today's children discuss and share ideas and find solutions to problems. It seems a different world to the classroom of old where children sat for long periods with their heads down. (1)........ How has such a huge change come about in just a single generation? Technology lies at the root.

In the past, many school subjects, like history, focused on learning and memorizing facts. Today, information is easier to obtain, and memorizing facts and details is not so important. In history, for example, lessons now concentrate on interpreting events and documents from the past. Class time is spent on discussion and project work.

Working collaboratively like this also prepares people for the modern working world. In a computerized age, many tasks are too complicated to be done by an individual. (2)........ Twenty people can brainstorm more ideas than just one person. Likewise, when today's students make decisions, they want to vote on the best solution. Everyone's opinion should be heard.

Working on teams is completely natural for so many teens and young adults (the so-called Generation Y). (3)........ Much of their time is spent online, interacting with other people via networking sites or an MMOG (a Massively Multiplayer Online Game, such as World of Warcraft). This requires people skills that easily translate to the workplace: how to allocate roles or negotiate to resolve a conflict. Generation Y wants feedback as well. A simple grade is not good enough for them. (4)........ That's normal if you're used to learning by questioning. Many young people will also give an employer their opinion from day one. They know that experience on its own is not enough to get the job done. Ideas and teamwork are more important.

One downside is that Generation Y also wants the constant change they are used to from online

SPEAKING & READING

1 **a** Work in groups. Read the quote. Do you agree with it? Why/Why not?

"Young people growing up in a digital age prefer working on teams to working alone."

b What is the connection between the quote and the images? Which image is most similar to the school you went to?

2 **a** Read the article quickly. Does the writer agree with the quote?

b Read the article again and answer the questions.

1 What is Generation Y?
2 What does the writer say about the style of education in image a?
3 What does the writer say about the style of education in image b?

3 Fill in blanks 1–6 in the article with sentences a–f.

a They want to know why things are right or wrong.
b Many people leave a great career for no particular reason.
c They've grown up doing it, in schools and online.
d On the other hand, older generations often don't understand Generation Y's ability to multitask.
e And to find creative solutions, working as a team is better.
f The days of the "chalk and talk teacher" are over.

4 **a** Work in pairs. Check your answers to 3. List four characteristics of Generation Y according to the article.

b Are you a member of Generation Y? Do you agree with the description of this group of people? Why/Why not?

environments. Often they will quit a job if it's not interesting enough to challenge them. (5) .... They often complain that "the job was just so boring," but it's unlikely their parents would have felt like this. (6) .... A boss is likely to be furious to discover a worker checking Facebook when an urgent deadline is due. But the world has changed. Some companies think that if they pay their employees enough money, everyone will be happy, but that's not true for Generation Y. They're not in it for the money. What they want is to feel part of a team and to have their voices heard.

b

Grammar

1 **a** Complete sentences 1–4 from the article with the words in the box.

boring	change	chaos	teens

1 I've never seen such .... !
2 How has such a huge .... come about in just a single generation?
3 Working on teams is completely natural for so many .... and young adults.
4 They often complain that "the job was just so ...."

b Check your answers in the article. Look at the words that follow *such*, *so* and *so many*. What part of speech is each one?

2 Match sentences 1–4 in 1a to uses a–d in the Grammar panel.

3 Complete the sentences with *so* or *such*.

1 My least favorite teacher was Mr. Cranston. He taught .... badly and was .... an impatient person.
2 Sometimes I'm too much of a perfectionist about my work. I spend .... much time checking it that I miss the deadline.
3 It was .... a complicated problem that our team didn't manage to solve it in time.
4 I obviously didn't spend enough time on the report. I've never received .... criticism for my work!

4 **a** Complete the sentences with your own ideas.

1 Nowadays, there's such a lot of...
2 Education today is so...
3 Young people today are such...

b Work in pairs. Take turns reading your sentences. Give more information to explain your ideas.

Notice *enough*

Notice how *enough* comes 1) after an adjective and 2) before a noun:

It's just not challenging enough.
They just don't pay enough money.

So/Such

We use *so* and *such* to add emphasis and intensify a description:

a) *so* + adjective/adverb:
The trip was so long. He speaks so slowly.

b) *so* + *much/many/little/few* + noun:
I have so much work to do this afternoon.

c) *such* + (*a/an*) + (adjective) + noun:
He's such a supportive manager.

d) *such* + noun to mean "this kind of":
I've never read such nonsense before.

Note: We often use *that* with *so/such* to talk about a result or consequence:
The job was so boring that I decided to quit.

See page 150 for grammar reference and more practice.

Speaking

1 Work in groups. Answer the questions.

1 Do you think it's easier to learn these things by yourself or in a group? Why?
- irregular verbs in a foreign language
- the basic skills of a sport
- how to assemble ready-to-assemble furniture
- how to play a musical instrument

2 Have you ever learned any of the things in 1? How did you learn it? Were you successful?

TUNE IN

1 Read the definition of "Murphy's Law." Do you have a phrase like this in your language? Do you agree with it?

> **Murphy's Law**
> an expression meaning "anything that can go wrong will go wrong"

2 **a** Work in pairs. Look at the image. What do you think has gone wrong?

b Have you had problems with a gadget or piece of equipment recently? What went wrong? How did you solve the problem?

3 11.5 Listen to conversations 1–4. Which conversation does the image show?

4 **a** Answer the questions for each conversation in 3.

1 What is person A's problem?
2 What does person B suggest?

b Listen again and check.

FOCUS ON LANGUAGE

5 Complete the sentences from the audio.

1 **It says on the box** that I .... them into this ....
2 **I've already tried** .... it in there.
3 **Is it meant to** .... the computer .... ?
4 **Have you tried** .... a media player?
5 **I've finally managed to** .... this shaver to work.
6 The instructions say **you're supposed to** .... the battery before you use it.

6 **a** Rewrite sentences 1–6 using one of the phrases in bold in 5.

1 What about turning it off then turning it on again?
Have you tried turning it off then turning it on again?
2 After a lot of effort I've succeeded in assembling the dresser.
3 It's written on the packaging that it'll work with any operating system.
4 The idea is that you attach the red wire to this switch here.
5 Does the computer usually make that sound?
6 I've attempted to call the helpline, but it was busy.

b 11.6 Listen and check.

> **Stress**
> 11.7 Listen to extracts 1–3. Underline the main stress.
> 1 Is it meant to slow the computer down?
> 2 I've finally managed to get this shaver to work!
> 3 You're supposed to charge the battery before you use it.
>
> Listen again and repeat with the correct stress.

OVER TO YOU

7 Work in pairs. Choose one of the situations. Make a list of four things that could go wrong and possible solutions to the problems.

- working out how to use a new cell phone
- assembling a lamp or ready-to-assemble furniture
- installing and playing a computer game
- setting up a new music system

8 **a** Work in pairs. Act out the situation in 7.

Student A

Tell your partner what has gone wrong and ask for help.

Student B

Listen to your partner and offer solutions.

b Switch roles. Prepare and act out another situation in 7.

TUNE IN

1 Work in groups. Discuss the questions.

- Do you have an e-reader? If so, what do you read on it? If not, why not?
- Do you prefer to use an e-reader, read on a computer or read printed books, magazines, etc.?
- What are the advantages and disadvantages of e-readers/reading on screen?

2 Look at the images. What do you think are the differences between the three e-readers?

3 **a** 11.8 Listen to two people discussing the e-readers. Number the images in the order they are mentioned.

b Answer the questions.

1 What is the name of each e-reader?
2 Which one does Colin decide to buy?

4 Listen again. Which e-reader...

1 is the largest?
2 has the most functions?
3 is the most expensive?
4 doesn't have a touch-sensitive screen?
5 can you bend?

PREPARE FOR TASK

5 **a** Work in pairs. Correct one mistake in each sentence.

1 On the one ~~side~~ *hand*, it's larger than other e-readers.
2 But on another hand, it's incredibly light and thin.
3 One thing to have in mind, though, is that you can only buy Kindle e-books through Amazon.
4 From all the options, it has the greatest functionality.
5 It has a touch-sensitive screen, when the Kindle uses buttons.
6 But for the downside, it costs more than the others.
7 Another thing in preference of the Skiff is that it's flexible.
8 They all seem to have the pros and cons.

b Check your answers in Transcript 11.8 on page 166.

6 Imagine you have to choose a present for a friend. Work with a partner who has the <u>same</u> role, A, B or C. Follow the instructions.

1 Student As, turn to page 160.
Student Bs, turn to page 161.
Student Cs, turn to page 163.

2 Discuss your present idea. Write down its pros and cons.
I like the rain poncho. Of all the options, it's the most practical.

TASK

7 **a** Work in groups of three, with one student from each A/B/C group. Take turns describing your present idea to the group.

b Discuss the pros and cons of the three items. Decide which item to buy as a present.

On the downside, it's not as much fun as the other two.

REPORT BACK

8 Tell the class which present your group chose and why. Which item was most popular in the class?

→ Go to Review D, Unit 11, p. 137 → Go to Writing Bank 6, p. 156

12 OUT OF THE ORDINARY

a

b

1 **a** Work in pairs. Look at the images and answer the questions.

1 What do the images have in common?
2 Which one (if any) appeals to you most? Why?

b Share your ideas with the class. Which image did most people like?

2 Work in pairs. Complete A in the KEY VOCABULARY PANEL. Use a dictionary to help you.

3 **a** 12.1 Listen to three people talking about the images. Match speakers 1–3 to images a–c.

b Listen again and answer the questions.

1 What time of day was it?
2 What made the moment so important?
3 What aspect of the story is shown in the images?

4 Work in pairs. Complete B in the KEY VOCABULARY PANEL.

5 **a** Think of an example of...

- a breathtaking or stunning view
- an awe-inspiring experience or sight
- an overwhelming emotion.

b Share your ideas with a partner. Use the adjectives and intensifiers in B.

6 **a** Match the extracts to the images.

1 I went on this incredible vacation. It was a once in a lifetime experience.
2 I stopped and stared. It just took my breath away.
3 There's this one memory that really stands out to me... an incredible memory.
4 When I got there I just couldn't believe my eyes.

b Complete C in the KEY VOCABULARY PANEL.

C

7 **a** Choose one of the expressions in C. Think of a story or an experience that you associate with the expression.

b Read the transcript on page 168 again and find expressions you can use in your story.

8 Work in pairs. Tell your partner your story.

Key Vocabulary

Experiences

A Times of day

- Match some of the words and phrases in the box to the images. Give reasons for your ideas.

dawn daybreak dusk early morning late afternoon midmorning sunrise sunset the dead of night twilight

- What do you associate with each of the times of day? Which time of day is your favorite? Why?
I always associate midmorning with a coffee break.

B Positive adjectives & intensifiers

- Read the definitions. Which speaker 1–3 used each adjective?

breathtaking, **stunning**	extremely impressive or beautiful
awe-inspiring	making you feel great respect and admiration
overwhelming	making you feel very strong emotions, often so strong that you cannot think or act

- Check your answers in Transcript 12.1 on page 168. What does each adjective describe?
- What other descriptive adjectives are used in the audio? Find examples of the intensifiers used with them (e.g., *truly*, *totally*).

Notice *awesome*
Awesome means extremely good. It is informal and is used in exclamations to express approval:
Awesome! / That's awesome!

C Expressions

- Complete the expressions without looking back at 6a. Then check your answers.

1 it took my .... away
2 I just couldn't .... my eyes
3 one memory that really .... out to me
4 a once in a .... experience

- PRACTICE REPORTING VERBS
- TALK ABOUT INTERESTING CHARACTERS

a

b

c

SPEAKING

1 a Work in pairs. Look at the images. What are the similarities and differences?

b Choose one of the men in the images. Imagine a life for him. Discuss the questions.

- Where is he? Why is he there?
- Is he alone, or is he waiting for someone?
- Why is he smiling? What is he thinking?

2 a Work with another pair. Share your ideas in 1b. Can they guess which man you chose? Do they agree with your impression of him?

b Answer the questions.

- What's the first thing you notice when you meet someone for the first time?
- Do you think you can always trust your first impressions? Why/Why not?

READING

1 a Read the blog post about first impressions. Answer the questions.

1. Who is the writer?
2. Who did she meet?
3. What did she think of him at first?
4. How did she feel about him at the end?

b Compare your answers with a partner's.

2 a Read the blog post again. Make a list of the things that drew the writer's attention to Carlos.

b Work in pairs. Compare your lists and discuss the questions.

- When did the writer first understand that Carlos was a con artist?
- When did you first suspect he might be a con artist?
- Do you think you would have been tricked by Carlos? Why/Why not?
- Look at images a–c again. Which one looks most like your impression of Carlos?

OVER Coffee

An interesting character

The first time I saw Carlos (as he called himself), he was standing at the bar, drinking an exotic-looking cocktail. It was eleven in the morning. I walked up and ordered coffee.

"That smells nice," he said, "Colombian?"

Now I don't usually like being approached by total strangers, but I'm a coffee lover, and there was something in his voice that made me look up. He sounded genuinely interested—and in the coffee, not in me.

We started up a conversation and found we had a lot in common. He claimed to be a lover of good coffee, a hater of time wasters, a fan of the simple things in life.

He suggested having lunch together at the hotel restaurant. I had no other plans and Carlos intrigued me, so I accepted. He insisted on paying for my coffee. I usually pay my own way, but with Carlos it was different. It was as if he had some kind of power over me.

At lunch he was charming. He spoke intelligently and interestingly about so many different topics. He explained that he was a writer, working on his next novel. I told him about the latest article I was writing and how little I got paid.

At that point he seemed to become bored and restless. An elderly woman came and sat at a nearby table, a wealthy permanent resident at the hotel. He excused himself and went over to her table. I don't know what he said, but she immediately invited him to join her.

I didn't see him again for a couple of days. Not until, that is, I heard a commotion in the reception area. I went out to see what was going on. The police were arresting Carlos. It turned out he was a con artist.

So, all that charm, all that fascinating conversation had been a con! As soon as he'd found out I wasn't a wealthy tourist but a poor journalist, he'd lost all interest. He'd moved on to his next victim.

The police accused Carlos of attempting to trick the old woman into giving him $10,000 to invest in a fictitious pension fund. And they congratulated her on spotting the trick. She looked very pleased with herself. He didn't. He suddenly looked ten years older. For a fleeting moment, I almost felt sorry for him.

Grammar

1 **a** Match the two halves of the sentences.

1 He later **explained**
2 He **claimed**
3 He **suggested**
4 He **insisted**
5 She **invited**
6 They **accused**
7 The police **congratulated**

a **having** lunch together.
b **him of attempting** to con the lady.
c **him to join** her.
d **on paying** for my coffee.
e **that** he was a writer.
f **the lady on spotting** the trick.
g **to be** a lover of good coffee.

b Check your answers in the text in **Reading 1a**.

2 Look again at the words and phrases in bold in 1a. Complete 1–7 in the Grammar panel with the correct verbs.

3 **a** Report the conversations using the verbs given.

1 **A** I think I'm going to be about twenty minutes late.
B Don't worry, I'll wait.

a He explained ....
b She promised ....

2 **A** Don't walk home through the park at night.
B OK, I won't. I'll get a taxi.

a They warned me not ....
b I agreed ....

3 **A** I'm so sorry I lost your book! I'll buy you another one!
B Why don't I just borrow one of yours instead?

a She apologized .... my book and offered ....
b I suggested ....

b Who do you think the speakers are in each conversation in 3a?

4 **a** Choose a reporting verb from three different sections, a–e, in the Grammar panel. Write a sentence with each reporting something you have said, or heard someone say, recently.

b Share your sentences in small groups. How many different reporting verbs did you use in total?

Pronunciation: Sentence stress

1 **a** 12.2 Listen to the sentences. Notice how the reporting verb is stressed in each one. What other words are stressed?

1 He in<u>sis</u>ted on paying the bill.
2 He <u>claimed</u> he was a coffee lover.
3 He de<u>nied</u> approaching the lady.
4 He <u>pro</u>mised to pay me back.

b Listen again and repeat.

Reporting Verbs

A Verb + *that* clause

When the reporting verb is in the past, the verb following *that* is often in the past, too:
He explained that he was a writer.

If the verb after *that* refers to a situation that is true in the present, we can also use a present form:
He warned me that conmen are difficult to spot.

Common verbs: *agree, claim, deny,* (1) ...., *insist, promise, recommend, reply, warn*

B Verb patterns

a Verb + *to* + infinitive: *I agreed to try.*
Common verbs: *agree,* (2) ...., *offer, promise*

b Verb + object + *to* + infinitive: *He advised me to be careful.*
Common verbs: *advise, ask,* (3) ...., *tell, warn*

c Verb + *-ing: He recommended going to the casino.*
Common verbs: *deny, recommend,* (4) ....

d Verb + preposition + *-ing: He apologized for spilling my coffee.*
Common verbs: (5) .... *(on), apologize (for)*

e Verb + object + preposition + *-ing: They blamed him for causing the accident.*
Common verbs: (6) .... *(of), blame (for),* (7) .... *(on)*

See page 151 for grammar reference and more practice.

Speaking & Listening

1 **a** 12.3 Listen to two people answering the question: *Have you ever met any interesting characters, people who were a little out of the ordinary?* Answer the questions for each speaker.

1 Where did he/she meet the person?
2 Why was the person interesting?

b Listen again. In which story, 1, 2 or both, do the people

1 communicate without speaking the same language?
2 have a long and interesting conversation?
3 share some food?
4 see each other on more than one occasion?
5 find a connection through music?

2 Think of an interesting character you have met. Prepare notes about the person to answer questions 1–2 in 1a.

3 **a** Work in pairs. Tell your partner about your interesting character. Are there any similarities between your stories?

b Report back to the class. Which person sounds the most interesting? Why?

12.2 NIGHT LIVES

- REVIEW PERFECT & CONTINUOUS TENSES
- TALK ABOUT UNUSUAL DAILY ROUTINES

a

b

SPEAKING & VOCABULARY: Night expressions

1 a Work in pairs. Look at images a–b and answer the questions.

- What time do you think it is?
- What are you usually doing at this time?
- What are the people in the photos doing?

b Write a list of jobs people do at night.

street cleaner, taxi driver...

2 a Compare your list with those of the rest of the class. Which jobs were mentioned most often? What was the most unusual job?

b Read the text. What do you think the writer's job is?

> How often do you **stay up** late? Ever stayed up **all night long**? Or maybe taken a ride on an **overnight bus** or **train**? I bet you didn't feel so great the next day, did you? For those of us who **work nights**, and go to bed **at the crack of dawn**, this exhausted feeling is all part of our everyday lives. I start my **night shift** at 11 p.m. and don't get home until 8 in the morning. It's usually quiet—most of the patients sleep comfortably through the night. At least I'm never **on call**—some of the doctors have to be available for 36 hours, trying to **get some sleep** between calls. Now *that's* exhausting!

3 Match the words and phrases in bold in 2b to definitions 1–8.

1. not go to bed *stay up*
2. ready to work whenever necessary ....
3. a period at work during the night in a place that stays open 24 hours ....
4. very early in the morning ....
5. do your job during the night ....
6. the whole night ....
7. a form of transportation that travels during the night ....
8. catch up on sleep ....

4 a Complete the questions with the phrases in bold in 2b.

1. If you've had a late night, do you ever try to .... later on the next day?
2. When was the last time you .... all night long?
3. Do you often get up .... dawn?
4. Have you ever been on an .... train?
5. Do you know anyone who has to be .... during the night?
6. If your boss offered you more money to work a ...., would you accept?
7. Are there any jobs where you typically have to .... that appeal to you?

b Work in pairs. Ask and answer the questions in 4a. Ask follow-up questions to find out more information.

LISTENING

1 a 12.4 Listen to two people talking about the people in images c–e on page 131. What does each person do at night, while the rest of the city is asleep?

b Listen again and complete the sentences in your own words.

1. David saw the video clips...
2. The clips are about...
3. Kris thinks the first person is...
4. The first person likes her job because...
5. The people in the second clip surprise the speakers because...
6. The people in the second clip like their job because...
7. People often stare at the third person because...
8. Kris thinks people won't pay him for his photos because...

2 a Work in pairs. Discuss the questions. Who...

- has the most exciting nights?
- meets the most people?
- finds their nights a welcome change from their daytime routine?

b Whose nightlife appeals to you most? Why?

Grammar

1 Match extracts a–e to the people in images c–e. What do the words in bold refer to?

a I'm glad someone is taking care of **them**.
b She's rescued hundreds of **them**.
c He's been doing **it** for six years.
d I guess he'll still be doing **it** when he's 100.
e He'd first fallen in love with **it** in the 1940s.

2 a Work in pairs. Look at the sentences in 1 and follow the instructions.

1 Underline all the past participles. Which auxiliary verb comes immediately before them?
2 Circle all the *-ing* verb forms. Which auxiliary verb comes immediately before them?
3 Which sentence contains both a past participle and an *-ing* form?

b Complete 1–5 in the Grammar Panel with sentences a–e in 1. Then match the examples in section A to uses a–h in section B.

3 a Choose the correct form to complete the sentences.

1 I *was working / had been working* really hard all week, so I was really glad the weekend *had arrived / had been arriving*.
2 *I've studied / I'm studying* more than usual at the moment because I have exams coming up next week.
3 I ran into an old friend when I *was walking / had walked* down the street.
4 *I'm passing / I've just passed* my driving test. What a great feeling!
5 This time next week, *I'll be lying / I'll have lain* on a beach in the sun!

b Compare your answers with a partner's. Have any of the sentences ever been true for you?

Yes, 3 happened to me a few months ago. I hadn't seen my ex-roommate for three years, and then there he was, coming out of a store in the mall

4 Write three questions using the prompts. Then ask and answer the questions with the same partner.

1 Have you ever...?
2 Do you think you will have... by the time...?
3 Had you ever thought about... before...?

Review: Perfect & Continuous

A Form

***have* + past participle** = a perfect tense
present perfect: (1) ....
past perfect: (2) ....
future perfect: *I'll have finished by the end of the day.*

be* + verb + *-ing = a continuous tense
present continuous: (3) ....
past continuous: *I found this when I was looking at some stuff on the Internet.*
future continuous: (4) ....

have* + *been* + verb + *-ing = perfect continuous tense
present perfect continuous: (5) ....
past perfect continuous: *He'd been working as a photographer since the 1960s.*

B Uses

An action that...

a) happened in the past (but we don't say when exactly). *She's rescued hundreds of them.*
b) started in the past and continues in the present.
c) will be in progress in the future.
d) was in progress before or up to a point in time in the past.
e) was in progress at a point in time in the past.
f) is in progress at the moment.
g) happened at some point before a given point in the past.
h) is going to finish before a certain point of time in the future.

See page 151 for grammar reference and more practice.

Speaking

1 a Work in pairs. Look at the questionnaire title. What do you think it is about?

Are you a night owl or an early bird?

b Write five questions for the questionnaire.

How late do you usually stay up at night?

2 Work with a partner from a different pair. Ask and answer your questions. Decide if your partner is a night owl or an early bird.

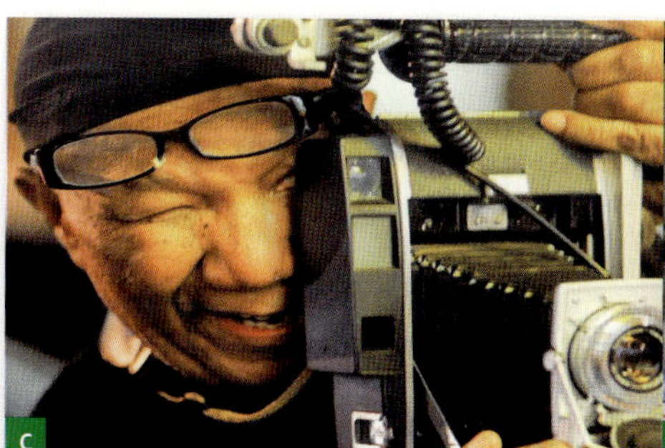
c

d

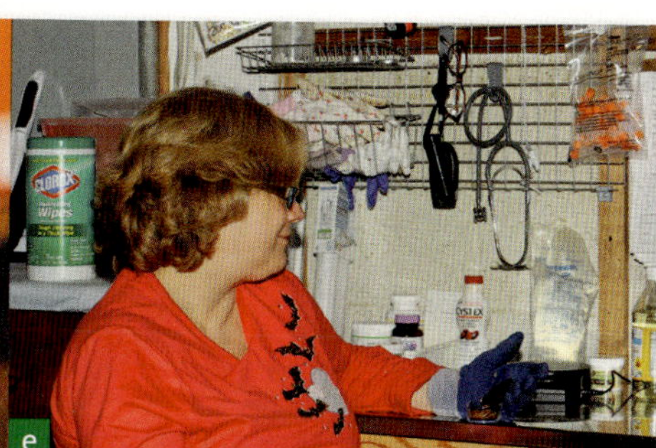
e

■ PRACTICE IDIOMATIC EXPRESSIONS
■ TALK ABOUT SPECIAL MOMENTS

READING & SPEAKING

1 a Work in small groups. Read the request a student posted on a social network. What is the link with the images? What experiences are shown in each photo?

b Read the replies 1–5 that her friends sent. Match them to images a–e. Check your answers in 1a.

Update status

PalominoVi
Hi! I need your help! Our teacher has given us this essay to write: "What are the simple pleasures in life? Why are they so important? Discuss, giving examples from your life and the lives of others."

So, I'm collecting examples of simple pleasures! A few words, a few sentences, anything you have to say would be much appreciated.

posted at 11:42 a.m. • Like | Comment

a

b

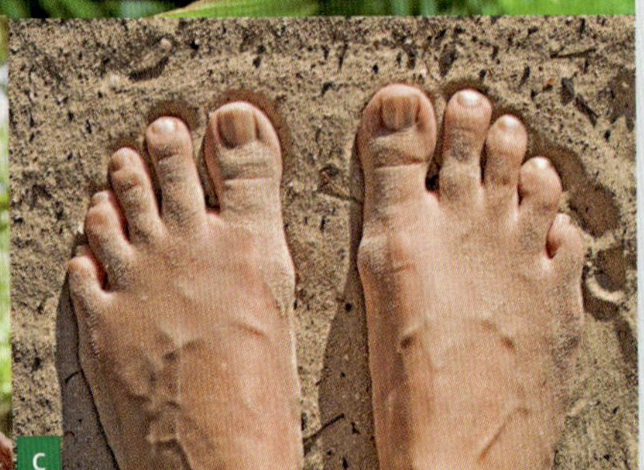

c

d

e

View all comments

cmclol 1
We saw a chameleon the other day. We'd never seen one before. We were on our bikes and almost ran over it! It was bright green, and it was making its way slowly across the road. As it scuttled away into the undergrowth it turned from bright green to mottled brown—amazing!

posted at 12:15 p.m. • Like

LAblogger 2
I love watching clouds. I like to just stop sometimes, take time out to look up, wherever I am and watch the clouds floating across the sky. It's just so relaxing. Almost hypnotizing.

posted at 2:24 p.m. • Like

Roslyn99 3
I love that first sip of coffee in the morning, when it's cold and dark outside. Somehow the first sip always tastes so good. And I stop for a second to hold the cup in my hand and let the steam rise onto my face.

posted at 6:30 p.m. • Like

Beach_babe 4
I love the feel of sand between my toes. That first moment when you take off your shoes and feel your feet sink into the sand. It always makes me smile!

posted at 6:42 p.m. • Like

Jacksonjo9 5
A simple pleasure? For me, it's that "aha!" moment when you understand something or you can do something for the first time, especially when you see that on a kid's face! Like the smile on Ellie's face the first time she rode her bike by herself.

posted at 8:53 p.m. • Like

2 **a** Work in pairs. Which reply/replies 1–5 describe(s)

- something the person has only done – or seen – once?
- something the person does as part of his/her daily routine?
- something the person does from time to time?

b Look at the categories in 2a. Think of a simple pleasure for each one, if possible. Take a minute to prepare the language you need to describe each experience.

3 Work in small groups. Share your experiences. Were there any similarities?

4 **a** Work as a group. Write a short answer to the question: What is a simple pleasure? Use no more than sixty words.

b Compare your answers with other groups'.

5 12.5 Read what the student wrote in her next update. Then listen to her summary. Is it similar to yours? In what ways is it similar/different?

Update status

PalominoVi
Thank you so much everybody for all your great replies—each and every one of them helped me with my essay. As part of the task, our teacher also asked us to record a short summary of our essay. Here's my recording. I hope you like it!

posted at 10:47 a.m. • Like | Comment

Vocabulary: Idiomatic expressions

1 Work in pairs. Look at extracts 1–6 from Transcript 12.5. Explain what the expressions in bold mean in your own words.

1. Small pleasures **come in all shapes and sizes**.
2. They make you **see** the **things** around you **in a different light**.
3. Make sure you **take the time to** stop...
4. ... and **make the most of** each and every special moment.
5. **That special "aha" moment,** when you finally understand something.
6. They make you **stop in your tracks**.

2 **a** Work in pairs. Match the expressions in bold in 1 to definitions a–f.

a suddenly forget about what you're doing at the time
b exist in many different forms
c you finally understand something after a period of confusion
d get everything you can from a situation
e think about something from a new angle
f do something slowly, without rushing

b Do you have any similar expressions in your language?

3 **a** Complete the questions with a word in bold in 1.

1. How often do you take the .... just to relax and be by yourself? Do you manage to make the .... of your free time? What do you usually do?
2. Can you remember a time when you had the "aha" .... when you managed to do or understand something?
3. Dreams come in all .... and .... What are yours usually about?

b Work in pairs. Ask and answer the questions in 3a.

Speaking

1 **a** Imagine you want to enter the competition below. Read the instructions and think of a special moment.

A Moment in Time

Enter our video competition and win two airline tickets to the destination of your choice.

Simply choose a special moment or a simple pleasure from the last month. Explain where you were and what happened. Tell us why it was important to you and how it made you feel. Then add your thoughts to a slideshow or a short video to last no more than two minutes.

b Work in pairs. Tell each other about the moment you chose.

- Explain where you were and what happened.
- Talk about how you felt.
- Discuss what kind of images you'd like to use to illustrate the moment.

2 Present your ideas to the class. Did the special moments you chose have anything in common?

TUNE IN

a

b

c

1 Work in pairs. Answer the questions.

- What is the relationship between the people in the images?
- What do you think they're talking about?
- When and where do you get together to chat with friends?
- What kinds of things do you talk about?

2 12.6 Listen to the conversation. Has something similar ever happened to anyone you know?

3 **a** Read a summary of the conversation. Find and correct eight more mistakes.

> A woman is telling a friend about an embarrassing situation that happened to her brother, Ray. Her friend ~~doesn't seem~~ *seems* very interested in the story. Yesterday, Ray and his girlfriend, Jackie, were going on vacation to Amsterdam. When they arrived at the airport, Ray realized that he had forgotten their passports. He had left them in his suitcase when he returned home from Paris the week before. They couldn't catch that flight and had to spend $450 on tickets for a later flight. The woman wants them to bring her back a Mexican *sombrero*.

b Listen again and check.

FOCUS ON LANGUAGE

4 **a** Read extracts 1–7. Are the expressions a) asking for more information, b) showing surprise or c) expressing sympathy?

1	Poor thing!	*c*	4	No way!	....
2	So what happened?	....	5	Go on.	....
3	You're joking!	....	6	You didn't!	....

b Listen to the conversation again. Mark the expressions in **4a** that you hear.

> ### Showing interest
> 12.7 Listen to the responses in **4a**. How does the listener use his/her voice to show interest and encourage the speaker to continue with the story?
>
> Listen again and repeat with the correct intonation.

5 **a** Read another story. After each line, write an expression that shows you are interested in the story.

1. I had an awful night last night.
   Oh no! What happened?
2. Well, I woke up in the middle of the night.
   ....
3. I could feel this... thing in my hair.
   ....
4. I jumped out of bed and turned on the light.
   ....
5. It was a massive cockroach!
   ....
6. I didn't know what to do, so I went into the living room to sleep on the sofa.
   ....
7. I couldn't get back to sleep for ages!
   ....

b Compare your conversations in pairs. Then act them out, using intonation to show interest.

OVER TO YOU

6 **a** Think of an interesting, surprising or embarrassing thing that has happened to you, or someone you know, recently. Prepare notes to help you tell your story.

b Work in pairs. Listen to each other's stories. Remember to sound interested and to prompt your partner to continue, wherever possible.

7 Report back to the class. Answer the questions.

- Did your listener show interest, sympathy or surprise? Did he/she react appropriately?
- Has anything similar happened to anyone you know?

TUNE IN

1 Work in small groups. Choose a story that you read or heard while studying this unit. Tell the group why you like it.

2 **a** Read another story. An image in this book reminded the writer of this event in his life. Can you find the image before the rest of the class?

Of all the times I've had to take an exam, there's one that really sticks in my mind. (1) ...., I lived in east Budapest, but the college was on the other side of the city. The exam was taking place in a hall near the college. I decided to leave early so that I could find it in plenty of time.
(2) ...., I used to go everywhere by subway. (3) ...., I went to the station feeling relaxed and confident. But (4) ...., I sensed trouble. (5) ...., the train stopped in the tunnel. (6) ...., we crawled into the station. The same thing happened between the next two stations—another ten minutes had gone by. And it kept happening! I was beginning to feel nervous. (7) .... the train reached Széll Kálmán Square, my stop. My watch said 10:07. I was late. I jumped off the train and ran as fast as I could. When I (8) .... got to the hall, my heart was beating like a drum. I sat down and looked at the clock. It was (9) .... 10:22.
Unsurprisingly, I've never written as fast as I did that day! I was on fire! I even finished a few minutes early. I wouldn't recommend being late to make you write fast on exams, but I did pass!

b Work in pairs. Have you ever been late for an important event? What happened?

3 Complete the story in **2a** with the time expressions in the box. Sometimes more than one answer is possible.

> now   finally   eventually
> within two minutes of getting on the train
> ten minutes later   on the day of the exam
> in those days   at the time
> before we'd arrived at the first station

PREPARE FOR TASK

4 Group phrases 1–8 according to whether you would see them at the beginning (B) or end (E) of a story.

1 Once, when I was just... years old... *B*
2 You can imagine how I felt! ....
3 So the next time you..., remember/don't forget to...! ....
4 One of the most memorable days of my life was when I... ....
5 Of all the times/places/people I've..., this has to be the most exciting/interesting/frightening, etc. ....
6 That's the last time I ever... ....
7 I'll never forget the day that... ....
8 It all turned out fine in the end. ....

5 **a** Read about a writing opportunity. How do you choose a story to write about?

b Choose an image and a story. Follow the instructions.

1 Decide how your story will begin and end.
2 If you like, use phrases from **4** to help tell your story.
3 Decide which time expressions from **3** may be useful.

TASK

6 Write your story. Organize it into at least three paragraphs, as follows.

1 **introduction**—where you were, what you were doing, any background information to set the scene
2 the **main events** in the story—what happened
3 a **conclusion**—what happened in the end, were there any consequences

REPORT BACK

7 **a** Read your story out loud. The rest of the class guesses which image from the book inspired it.

b Decide whose story a) was the funniest, b) was the most unusual or surprising or c) fitted the image best.

➜ Go to Review D, Unit 12, p. 138

VOCABULARY

Materials

1 Work in pairs. Think of two items made from each material in the box.

cotton leather nylon pine
rubber silk steel wool

cotton – sheets, clothes...

Adjective order

2 **a** Work in pairs. Student A, look at the image below. Student B, turn to page 162. Imagine this is your store. Follow the instructions.

Take turns asking for three items in your partner's store. Use at least three adjectives to describe each one. How quickly can your partner identify the item?

How much is the large blue plastic thing on the right?

Business & finance

3 **a** Complete the sentences with the correct form of the words in the box.

fork out get into repay rip off run

1 What's the most expensive thing you've ever .... a lot of money for?
2 Do you know anyone who's been .... recently? What happened?
3 Would you like to .... your own business? Why/Why not?
4 Why do people .... debt with credit cards?
5 What's the best way to .... a loan?

b Work in pairs. Ask and answer the questions.

GRAMMAR

Either... or/Neither... nor

1 **a** Work in pairs. Complete the sentences so they are true for your country/town.

1 For breakfast, people either...
2 In my neighborhood, there's neither...
3 The most interesting thing to do there is either...
4 People here neither...

b Report back to the class. What was the most surprising information in 1a?

Articles

2 Complete the definition with *a/an*, *the* or ø (no article).

nylon *(n)* this is .... artificial material invented in 1935 by Wallace Carruthers, ... American scientist. It remains one of .... most popular kinds of .... fabric in .... world.

3 **a** Work in pairs. Find three new words that you've learned in this book. Write definitions for them, similar to the one in 2.

b Work with another pair. Read your definitions. Can they guess/remember the words?

FUNCTIONAL LANGUAGE

Arranging for a service

1 **a** R18 Listen to someone arranging for a service. Answer the questions.

1 What does the man need an estimate for?
2 When is someone going to visit his house?
3 What's his budget for the job?
4 How much deposit would he need to pay?

b Put the words in order to complete the sentences. Listen again and check.

1 an / get / for / like / to / estimate / I'd / updating my bathroom.
2 for / arrange / I / someone / could / to come over ?
3 the / for / job / a / have / you / do / budget ?
4 need / I / deposit / pay / to / will / a ?
5 if / discount / a / cash / there / is / pay / I ?

LOOKING BACK

- Which topics in this unit would you like to know more about?
- Is there anything that you want to look at again?
- Think of five new phrases you have learned to talk about shopping and finance.

VOCABULARY

Talking about ideas & inventions

1 **a** Match the words to form compound nouns and adjectives.

1 touch-	a through
2 draw	b held
3 light	c edge
4 high-	d sensitive
5 cutting-	e weight
6 break	f tech
7 hand	g back

b Which words in 1a are a) nouns? b) adjectives?

2 Work in pairs. Use some of the words in 1a to describe your belongings.

I love my mountain bike – it's lightweight and fast.

3 Use the words in the box and some of the words in 1a to complete the text.

adopters	came	commercial	figured
gimmick	~~inspirational~~	launched	struck

Dyson Bagless Vacuum Cleaners:

an (1) *inspirational* idea

James Dyson (2) .... up with the idea for a better vacuum cleaner in the late 1970s. It (3) .... him that existing machines had a major (4) ....: they kept losing suction power as the bag filled up. Then he had a flash of inspiration: he (5) .... out how to use his (6) .... "cyclone technology" from a previous invention to get around the problem. Five years and over 5,000 prototypes later, Dyson's machine was ready. However, (7) .... success didn't come immediately. No one was interested in his product, describing it as a (8) .... The (9) .... came when he (10) .... it himself. Although it cost $2,000, early (11) .... loved it and turned the "Dyson" into a status symbol. Today, more than 20 million machines have been sold.

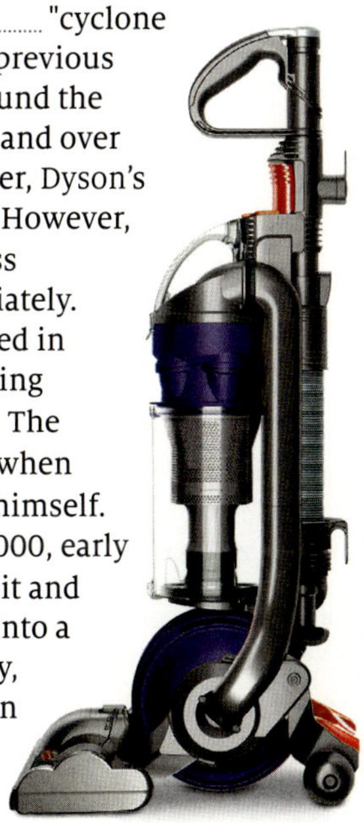

GRAMMAR

Relative clauses

1 **a** Join the sentences, using a relative pronoun. Omit the relative pronoun where possible.

1. This is the novel. I bought it online. *This is the novel I bought online.*
2. I'm reading it on my new iPad. It's generally good but has some drawbacks.
3. It has a reflective screen. This makes it hard to read outside.
4. Anyway, the story is about a Dutch man. He falls in love with a Japanese midwife.
5. Unfortunately, I've lost the cable for my iPad. This means I'll have to wait three weeks to read the end!

b R19 Listen and check your answers.

2 **a** Write a short summary (about forty words) of a book you have read recently, or a TV show/movie you have seen. Use relative clauses.

I read Snowdrops, *which was nominated for the Booker Prize. It's about a British lawyer who lives in Moscow...*

b Work in pairs. Read each other's summaries. Would you like to read the book or watch the show/movie? Why/Why not?

So/Such

3 **a** Complete the speech with *such*, *so* or *that*.

And now, for the prizes! There were (1) .... many excellent inventions in this year's competition. We've never had (2) .... good entries! They're all (3) .... original. In fact, the entries were of (4) .... a high standard (5) .... we've decided to give prizes to three different inventions...

b Where/When might you hear a speech like this?

FUNCTIONAL LANGUAGE

Dealing with technical problems

1 R20 Listen and complete the sentences.

1. I've already tried ....
2. Have you tried .... ?
3. The instruction manual says ....
4. Is it meant to .... ?
5. I haven't managed to ....

LOOKING BACK

- Think of six new words or phrases you've learned to talk about technology and innovations.
- Which speaking activity did you find the most difficult? Why?
- Which lesson motivated you most? Why?

VOCABULARY

Times of day

1 a Match the times of the day to the letters on the timeline.

dawn/daybreak   late afternoon   noon
sunrise   sunset   the dead of night

b Work in pairs. Tell your partner what you were doing yesterday at the times in 1a.

I was in the supermarket around noon.

Describing experiences

2 Complete the expressions.

1 Watch the solar eclipse in Antarctica with IceTour Cruises! Don't miss this o*n c e* in a l.................... e.....................!
2 After the birth of our daughter, my view on life changed and I began to see t........... in a d.................. l.......... .
3 In Nepal we visited Pokhara. Some of the views looking across to the Himalayas are totally F.......................... .
4 Visiting my grandparents in Australia when I was five is one memory that really s............ o...... t .... me.
5 I couldn't b............. m.... e........ when I saw the hotel we were staying in. It looked like a palace.

3 a Prepare brief notes on...

1 a stunning view you have seen.
2 an experience you probably won't repeat in your lifetime.
3 the last time you were overwhelmed by emotion.
4 an event that made you see things in a different light.

b Work in pairs. Take turns describing your experiences in 3a. Ask questions to find out more information.

Night expressions

4 a Number the lines of text in order from 1–10.

.... our everyday lives. I start my night
.... nights and go to bed at the crack of
.... up late? Ever stayed up all night
.... shift at 11 p.m. and finish at 8 a.m. At least I'm never on
...*1*... How often do you stay
.... dawn, this exhausted feeling is all part of
.... some sleep between calls. Now *that's* exhausting!
.... long? Or maybe riding on an overnight
.... call, like some doctors. They have to try and get
.... bus or train? For those of us who work

b Check your answers in **SPEAKING & VOCABULARY 2b** on page 130.

GRAMMAR

Reporting verbs

1 a R21 Listen to two conversations. Answer the questions.

1 What are the relationships between the three people?
2 Why is the man in conversation 1 (Michael) angry?
3 Why do Darren and Katy go for a meal?

b Listen again. Number the actions in order from 1–8.

.... Darren offered...
.... Darren denied...
.... Darren insisted...
.... Darren explained...
...*1*... Michael accused...
.... Katy promised...
.... Katy congratulated...
.... Katy suggested...

2 a Work in pairs. Compare your answers in 1b. Then complete the sentences.

Michael accused Darren of stealing the money.

b Check your answers in Transcript R21 on page 168.

FUNCTIONAL LANGUAGE

Showing interest

1 a R22 Listen to one side of a phone conversation. What's the gossip?

b Listen again. Write the other side of the phone conversation.

2 Work in pairs. Using your notes in 1b and Transcript R22 on page 168, act out the conversation.

LOOKING BACK

- Do you know anyone who has done anything out of the ordinary recently? Tell a partner.
- What was your favorite lesson in this unit? What did you like about it?
- Choose five words or expressions from the unit you would like to remember.

SPEAKING & READING

1 Work in pairs. Look at the image of a learner practicing English. Answer the questions.

1 What do you think he's doing?
2 Would you call this studying? Why/Why not?
3 What have you been doing recently to practice your English outside class?

2 **a** Read the report. Label the chart, a–h, with the underlined activities.

Report: Students' Independent Learning Practices

Introduction: We carried (1) .... a survey among the students at school concerning their attitudes toward learning English outside the classroom. Our aim was to share good learning practices before the end of the semester.

Independent Study: When asked how much they study outside class, most (2) .... the 167 respondents claimed (3) .... do between two and five hours a week. Popular activities include using the workbook, (4) .... was almost universal, and listening to music with the lyrics, which was enjoyed (5) .... just under half the students.

Without exception, students use the Internet to practice listening and reading. There were (6) .... many different ways to do this (7) .... we cannot explain them here. Surprisingly, over 10% of us also manage (8) .... practice speaking online, in forums and language exchange sites.

Vacation Plans: Sadly, only two people have borrowed a book from the library. However, the vast majority of students plan to practice English over vacation, (9) .... studying at home (about three quarters) or even traveling to an English-speaking country (16 people).

Problems: Students seem motivated and have good ideas (10) .... practicing listening and speaking skills. (11) .... the downside, many are worried that once classes are over, they won't dedicate (12) .... time to English.

Recommendations: We think that students should...

a ....
b ....
c *do 2–5 hours a week*
d ....
e ....
f ....
g ....
h *borrow book*

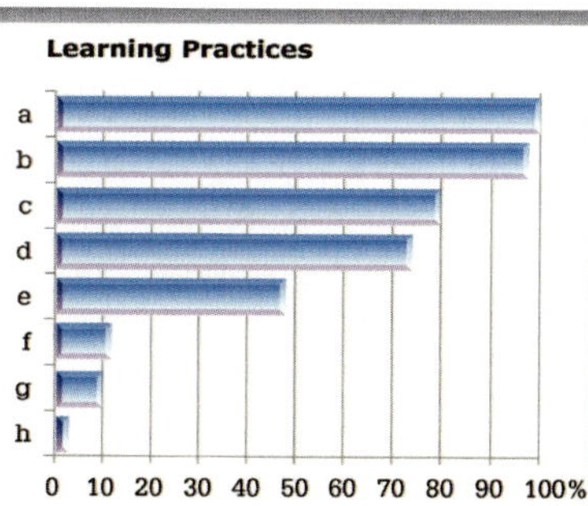

b Work in pairs. Which activity in 2a do you think is the best independent learning practice? Why?

3 Complete the text with the words in the box.

by either enough for of on out so that to (x2) which

WRITING & SPEAKING

4 **a** Work in pairs. What recommendations do you think the report will make? Write three practical steps for practicing and improving English over vacation.

b Share your recommendations in groups. Write down any ideas from other pairs that you think are useful.

5 Choose the best ideas for you from the list in 4. How are you going to keep improving? Tell your partner your plans.

QUICK CHECK

Complete the checklist below.

Can you...	Yes, I can.	Yes, more or less.	I need to look again.
1 talk about retail and finance and describe goods?	☐	☐	☐
2 discuss modern innovations and gadgets?	☐	☐	☐
3 describe memorable experiences?	☐	☐	☐
4 report what people say?	☐	☐	☐
5 arrange to have a service done for you?	☐	☐	☐
6 show interest in what people are saying?	☐	☐	☐
7 write a report on the findings of a survey?	☐	☐	☐
8 discuss the pros and cons of an issue?	☐	☐	☐

Compare your answers with a partner's.

- What else do you know now after studying units 10–12?
- Do you need to look again at any of the sections?
- Do you need any extra help from your teacher?

7.1 Past modals: *should have/could have*

We form past modals with a modal verb + *have* + past participle.

We use *should(n't)* + *have* + past participle

1 to criticize a past action:

You shouldn't have complained to your boss.

2 to express regret about a past action, or suggest a better alternative:

We should have stayed at the Continental Hotel, not the Atlantic.

We use *could(n't)* + *have* + past participle to talk about possibility in the past:

I didn't know you were coming to the station, too. I could have given you a lift.

Nick couldn't have gone on the trip last week because he had the flu.

7.2 Past modals: speculation & deduction

We can use past modals to speculate or make guesses about past events or situations.

When we are sure something happened, we use *must* + *have* + past participle:

The streets are soaking wet. It must have rained last night.

When we think something possibly happened, we use *could/may/might* + *have* + past participle:

There's a broken cup on the floor. Someone could have dropped it. The cat might have knocked it over. It may have fallen off the shelf.

When we think something possibly didn't happen, we use *may/might not* + *have* + past participle:

Jim didn't come to the meeting. He may not have known about it.

Leticia hasn't phoned me yet. She might not have read my e-mail.

Do not contract *may not have*:

NOT *He ~~mayn't~~ have had time to go.*

When we are sure something didn't happen, we use *can't* + *have* + past participle:

I just passed Bernie in the street. He can't have seen me because he didn't say hello.

We can also use *couldn't have* + past participle when we are sure something didn't happen:

Karen couldn't have been at the party last night. I was there all evening and I didn't see her.

7.1

Complete the sentences using *should(n't) have/could(n't) have* and the prompts.

1 I wanted to invite Tom to the party, but he was away on a trip.
.... *(Tom / come / to the party)*

2 I argued with my sister yesterday. Now I regret it.
.... *(I / argue / with her)*

3 I parked my car on the sidewalk, and now I have a parking ticket!
.... *(I / park / in the parking lot)*

4 If you hadn't helped me study, I wouldn't have passed the exam.
.... *(I / pass / the exam / without your help)*

5 If I'd known you needed to borrow $20, I would have helped you.
.... *(I / lend / you / $20)*

7.2

Choose the correct options to complete the conversation.

Marti Hi Lola!

Lo99 Hey!

Marti How are you? I wanted to talk to you yesterday but you (1)*can't / might not* have been online—I didn't see your name on the website.

Lo99 No, I had a crazy day! When I woke up, there was a strange smell in the house. I went into the kitchen and the gas was on. I thought Pete (2)*must / may* have forgotten to turn the stove off, but I wasn't sure.

Marti But that's really dangerous!

Lo99 I know! I was really angry! But he said it was my fault—that I (3)*can't / must* have left it on.

Marti You? Is that possible?

Lo99 No! I (4)*couldn't / might not* have done it because I didn't cook yesterday.

Marti There's another possibility—your stove (5)*might / must* have been broken.

Lo99 Well, finally we called the gas company... an hour later, someone came to repair it. It was all so quick—they (6)*must / could* have thought it was an emergency!

Marti Hmm... 😐 Sounds like you had a lucky escape!

Done

8.1 *If* sentences: imagined situations (1)

Use *if* + past simple to describe imagined situations in the present or future. Use *would/could/might* + infinitive for the imagined consequence:

If unemployment wasn't so high, there might be less crime. (present)

If I found $100 in the street, I'd (I would) hand it to the police. (future)

We can use *was* or *were* with *I/she/he/it* to talk about an imagined situation in the present or future. *Were* is usually used in more formal situations:

If I was you, I'd phone the police.

If he were older, he would receive a prison sentence.

Use *if* + past perfect to describe imagined situations in the past. Use *would have/might have/could have* + infinitive for the imagined consequence:

If I hadn't left my wallet on the train, it wouldn't have been stolen.
They could have stolen more if they'd had more time.

8.2 Wishes & regrets

I wish.../If only...

Use *I wish/If only* +

past simple to talk about	a situation in the **present** that we want to be different: *I wish/If only I had a car.* (= I don't have a car.)
past perfect to talk about	a situation in the **past** that we want to be different: *I wish/If only I hadn't forgotten my key.* (= I forgot my key.)
could to talk about	a **present** fact with *can/can't* that we want to be different: *I wish/If only I could go out tonight!* (= I can't go out tonight.)

We can also use *I wish/If only* + *would* when we want something to change, or when we want someone to do something:

If only it would stop raining! I want to go out for a walk.

I wish Laura would turn the TV down. It's so loud!

8.3 *If* sentences: imagined situations (2), mixed time frames

If sentences can have mixed time frames. This means that the time in the *if* clause can be different from the time in the result clause.

Past & present

An imagined situation in the past (*if* + past perfect) can have an imagined consequence in the present (*would/could/might* + infinitive):

If he hadn't made friends with the wrong people, he wouldn't/might not be in court today.

Present & past

An imagined situation in the present (*if* + past simple) can have an imagined consequence in the past (*would/could/might* + *have* + past participle):

If he had more respect for authority, he wouldn't/might not have gone to prison.

8.1

a Match the two halves of the sentences.

1 If we .... (*remember*) to lock the windows,
2 His life .... (*be*) very different
3 Downtown .... (*look*) much better
4 If I .... (*learn*) some karate,
5 If someone .... (*see*) the attack,
6 If she .... (*not/tell*) so many lies,

a I .... (*feel*) much safer walking home alone.
b we .... (*believe*) her story about last night.
c if he .... (*not/join*) that gang.
d the burglar .... (*not/get*) into the house.
e if there .... (*not/be*) so much graffiti.
f they .... (*catch*) the mugger.

b Complete the sentences with the correct form of the words in parentheses. Use *could (have)* and *might (have)* at least once. More than one answer may be possible.

8.2

Correct the mistakes in the sentences. One sentence is already correct.

1 If only we had know that our tour guide was a fraud!
2 I wish there aren't so many pickpockets working in the station.
3 I wish you weren't so naive sometimes.
4 I wish I can help you, but there's nothing I can do.
5 If only Jeff told us the truth last week.

8.3

Read the sentences. Rewrite them using a mixed conditional sentence.

1 I didn't sleep well last night, so I feel terrible today.
If I ....
....

2 Someone stole my wallet. Now I have to cancel my credit card.
If my ....
....

3 Fran didn't know the e-mail was a scam because she doesn't speak the local language.
If Fran ....
....

9.1 Adding emphasis: cleft sentences

We use cleft sentences to emphasize the main topic of a sentence. The normal word order of the sentence changes:

Public speaking makes me nervous.
It's public speaking that makes me nervous.

We can form cleft sentences using:

1 *It's* + main topic + *that* + information about topic:
I'm not afraid of spiders. It's snakes that really frighten me!

2 *The thing that* / *The reason why* + information about topic + *is* + main topic:
The thing that annoys me most is being interrupted.
The reason why I hate interviews is that I have to wear a suit.
We can replace *thing* with other words or phrases:
The part of the exam that I hate the most is getting started!

3 *What* + information about topic + *is* + main topic:
What makes me nervous is public speaking.

We can also use cleft sentences with *was:*
The worst interview that I've ever done was the one for my first job.

9.2 Making comparisons

To make comparisons, we can use...

1 comparative + *and* + comparative:
Fatima works out every day. She's getting slimmer and slimmer.

2 *the* + comparative... + *the* + comparative...
We use this structure when one thing (in the second part of the sentence) is dependent on another thing (in the first part of the sentence):
The more I train, the faster I run. (= I can run faster because I have done more training.)

3 superlative + present perfect
We use this structure to compare a person or event with our experience up to now:
The furthest I've ever run is 25 kilometers. (= I have never run further than this.)

9.3 Modifying comparisons

We can use modifiers like *a little, much,* etc. with comparative adjectives to show the level of difference between the things we are comparing.

If there is a big difference between the things, use *much, far more* or *a lot:*
Living in a big city is a lot more expensive than living in a small town.

We can also use *nowhere near/not nearly* + *as* + adjective + *as* to show a big difference:
Living here is nowhere near as expensive as living in New York. (= it's a lot cheaper to live here)

If there is a small difference between the things, use *a little bit, a little* or *slightly*:
My house a little bigger than the one next door.

We can also use *not quite as* + adjective + *as* to show a small difference:
My house isn't quite as big as the one next door. (= it's nearly the same size)

If there is no difference between the things, use *just as* + adjective + *as*:
My house is just as big as the one next door. (= they are the same size)

In questions and negatives, use *any* + comparative adjective:
Is this house any cheaper than that one?
This house isn't any cheaper than that one.

9.1

a Read the paragraph about Jason's job interview. Put the words in the correct order to complete the sentences.

> **My Interview Nightmare!**
> Once, I was half an hour late for a job interview because my train was delayed. Unfortunately, my cell phone battery had gone dead, so I couldn't call the company to tell them! When I finally arrived, the interviewer was very understanding. I couldn't believe it when they told me I had gotten the job!

1 .... *(was / it / a / with transportation / that / problem)* made Jason late.
2 .... *(reason / Jason / why / couldn't / was / the / call / that / company / the)* his cell phone's battery had gone dead.
3 .... *(surprising / what / is / that / is)* Jason got the job!

b Write five sentences describing an interview nightmare. Include at least two cleft sentences.

9.2

Complete the dialogue using the correct comparative form of the adjectives in parentheses.

A Hi Carl. I didn't know you were a member of this gym.
B Well, I'm training for a charity marathon and it's the (1) .... *(good)* gym I've found in the area.
A That's great. I'm just starting, but the (2) .... *(long)* I exercise, the (3) .... *(tired)* I get!
B OK, but you'll get used to it. You'll get (4) .... *(fit)* and (5) .... *(fit)* if you keep coming here.
A Before now, my only exercise was walking the dog.
B Well, the more you exercise, the (6) .... *(good)* you'll feel!

9.3

a Choose the correct option to complete the sentences.

> **I'm 22 and unemployed. I think having a degree means it's only (1)*slightly / much* easier to find a job. So is what you know (2)*as / any more* important than who you know?**
> **Sandra** Posted 11:14 a.m.
>
> Personally, I think it's all about meeting the right people. Contacts are (3)*far / a little* more important than qualifications.
>
> A college degree is nowhere (4)*near / nearly* as important as you might think. Employers are (5)*quite / just* as interested in relevant work experience.
>
> Qualifications may not be (6)*any / quite* as important in the creative industries, but that's not true for doctors.

b Write a reply to Sandra's question in **a**. Use comparative adjectives and modifiers.

10.1 *Either... or/Neither... nor*

We use *either... or* and *neither... nor* to talk about two or more different things. We use *either... or* in positive sentences to mean "one or the other." We use *neither... nor* in negative sentences to mean "not one and not the other."

Either... or/neither... nor can be used with

- two or more nouns: *We're going to buy either a sofa or an armchair for the living room.*
- two or more adjectives: *The sofa is available in either white, black or red.*
- two or more linked clauses: *You can either pay in cash or use your credit card.*
- two or more separate clauses: *Either we buy the sofa here or we look for a better deal online.*

We can also use *either/neither* alone:

Which dress do you like, the red one or the black one? Neither. I prefer this one, in blue.

Do you want to try on the black dress or the red dress? Either. I like them both.

10.2 Articles

	Basic uses	Other uses
a/an	with singular countable nouns	• when we mention someone/something for the first time • when we talk about jobs or professions: *I'm a salesperson.* • when we talk about what someone/ something is or is like: *eBay is an online auction site. Shane is a really generous person.*
the	with uncountable and countable nouns	• to talk about a specific person/thing • when someone/something has already been mentioned • when a person/thing is the only one in the context (and it is obvious what we are referring to): *I bought a newspaper at the station.* (= the station in this town) • when we talk about something that is unique in the world: *I bought these shoes on the Internet.* • with some adjectives to talk about a specific group of people: *the young, the elderly, the French* • with ordinal numbers and superlatives: *It's the best place to buy fruit and vegetables.* • with the names of deserts, rivers, mountain ranges and country names that include a political label (e.g., *state, republic*) • with the names of specific hotels, museums and art galleries
no article	with uncountable nouns and plural countable nouns	• when we talk about general or abstract things: *Online shopping is really convenient.* • with the names of continents, regions, most countries, individual mountains and lakes

We do not usually use *the* with parts of the body. We use *my, his,* etc.

10.1

a Complete the sentences with *either... or/neither... nor.*

1 I **always** eat a good meal during the day, ... at **lunchtime** .... **in the evening**.

2 If I go out for a meal, I like to eat .... **Chinese** .... **Thai** food.

3 When I need to buy food, I go .... to **the market** .... to **the local stores near my house**.

4 I rarely **cook at home**. I find **cooking** .... **interesting** .... **enjoyable**.

b Rewrite the phrases in bold so the sentences are true for you.

10.2

a Correct the sentences. Two sentences are already correct.

1 I think you've broken the ankle and you need to go to the hospital.

2 The night market is best market in the city.

3 I have a very strange ambition—I want to cross Sahara on a motorcycle.

4 Everyone knows that eating the fruit and vegetables is good for you.

5 I've bought a new camera. It's the one I found on that auction site on the Internet.

6 If you get room at the Bavaria Hotel, you'll have a fantastic view of Alps.

7 Fran's staying at home today because she has a cold.

8 I heard unusual story on the radio this morning.

b Add articles to the text where necessary.

Hi Andy,

How's life? Everything's OK with me, although I'm looking for job at the moment. I spent summer working with my uncle, because he has yacht here in Ukraine. We were taking tourists sailing around Black Sea. It's been fun, but now all tourists are going home, and I don't have any work. I'm thinking of going to USA, like you, and trying to work in tourism industry there. As you know, I love working with boats, but I'm happy to do anything. I was wondering whether I could find work in hotel, maybe even Foxton Hotel, like you. Do you think I should send my CV to manager?

If there isn't job there for me, I'll take a look on the Internet, too. Can you recommend website where I can search for international jobs?

Thanks—and talk to you soon!

Nikolay

11.1 Relative clauses

We use relative clauses to give information about a person or thing. In relative clauses, we use *who* to talk about people, *that* or *which* to talk about things, *where* to talk about places or *whose* to talk about possession.

Defining relative clauses

Defining relative clauses explain which person/thing is being described.

I need to speak to someone who understands computers. (*who understands computers* explains which kind of person)

In a defining relative clause, we can use *that* to replace *who*. We can also omit *who* or *that* if they are the object of the verb in the relative clause:

This is the website that I use to study English. (*the website* is the object of the relative clause)

This is the website that has English grammar exercises. (*the website* is the subject of the relative clause so *that* cannot be omitted)

Nondefining relative clauses

Nondefining relative clauses give extra information about the person/thing being described. They are usually separated from the rest of the sentence by commas:

The website, which was started by a teacher, is great for English students.

A nondefining relative clause can give extra information about a whole sentence. In this case it begins with *which*:

The website lets you record yourself speaking English, which is useful.

In nondefining relative clauses we do not use *that* and we cannot omit the relative pronoun.

11.2 *So/Such*

So

We use *so* with adjectives and adverbs to make their meaning stronger:

Technology is so important to our lives these days.

Technology changes so quickly these days.

So can also intensify the meaning of quantifiers, e.g., *much, many, few.* We use *so* + quantifier + noun:

My children own so many gadgets!

Note: We use *such* + *a lot (of)*:

Aisha spends such a lot of time online.

Such

We use *such (a)* + adjective + noun to make a description stronger. We use *such a* with singular countable nouns:

Technology is such an important part of our lives these days.

We use *such* with plural countable nouns and uncountable nouns:

That company makes such reliable laptops.

These new smartphones use such sophisticated technology.

We sometimes use *such a* + noun to intensify the meaning of a noun:

I bought this laptop on sale. It was such a bargain! (= it was a very good bargain)

We can also use *such* + noun to mean "this type of":

Such technology will soon be available to the public. (= this kind of technology)

11.1

a Cross out the word in bold, if possible.

1 I want to find a lawyer **who** speaks English.
2 I love the pictures **that** your mom bought for the living room.
3 Last year, there was a terrible blizzard **that** closed all the roads.
4 Have you seen the story **that** Giselle put on her website?
5 The police officer **who** we spoke to was really helpful.

b Complete the sentences with *who, whose, which* or *that*. In which sentence can the relative pronoun be omitted?

1 The weather was sunny yesterday, ... was nice.
2 That's the designer .... invention won an innovation award.
3 Professor Clay, ... taught me in college, was on the news today!
4 Computer science is a subject .... I'd like to know more about.
5 The city art gallery, ... is free, has a lot of interesting pictures.

11.2

a Complete the sentences with *so* or *such (a/an)*.

1 Steve Jobs, who died in 2011, was .... influential person within the technology industry.
2 He helped design and launch .... many great products like the iPhone and iPad.
3 .... products are sold all over the world and have made Apple a very successful company.
4 Jobs's designs show .... attention to detail; every button or switch is the perfect size and shape!
5 I think Jobs is .... inspiration; he worked .... hard to achieve his goals.

b Write three sentences describing a person you admire. Use *so* and *such (a/an)*.

12.1 Reporting verbs

Verb + infinitive

Some reporting verbs (e.g., *agree, claim, offer, refuse, promise*) are followed by *to* + infinitive: *He promised to do better the next time.*

Some reporting verbs (e.g., *advise, ask, invite, tell, remind, encourage, warn*) are followed by object + *to* + infinitive: *She asked me to go.*

Verb + -*ing*

Some reporting verbs (e.g., *deny, recommend, suggest*) are followed by the -*ing* form: *She recommended having dinner at the hotel.*

Verbs followed by a preposition (e.g., *insist on, apologize for, accuse of*), or an object and a preposition (e.g., *blame for, congratulate on*) are followed by the -*ing* form: *She insisted on paying.*

We form the negative of these structures using *not* (before the infinitive or -*ing* form): *She apologized for not calling me. He warned the children not to eat too much candy.*

Verb + *that* + clause

Many reporting verbs can be followed by *that* + clause. *That* can be omitted in informal English: *They explained (that) they needed more time.*

12.2 Review: perfect & continuous

Perfect tenses

We form perfect tenses with a form of *have* + past participle.

present perfect	an action/event that happened at some point in the past: *My brother has been to India twice.*
past perfect	an action/event that happened at some point before a given point in the past: *He had visited a lot of other countries before he decided to go to India.*
future perfect	an action/event that is going to finish before a given point in the future: *After his next trip, he'll have been to India three times.*

Continuous tenses

We form continuous tenses with a form of *be* + -*ing*.

present continuous	an action/event that is in progress now: *My brother is traveling around India at the moment.*
past continuous	an action/event that was in progress at a point in the past: *He became interested in India while he was studying in college.*
future continuous	an action/event that will be in progress at a point in the future: *I'm sure he'll still be going to India when he's an old man.*

Perfect continuous tenses

We form perfect continuous tenses with a form of *have* + *been* + -*ing*.

present perfect continuous	an action/event that started in the past and is still in progress now: *My brother has been traveling for two months.*
past perfect continuous	an action/event that was in progress before or up to a point in the past: *Before he went traveling he had been working for two years as a teacher.*

12.1

a Choose the correct options.

My friend Josh told me that he (1)*has / had* to take his driving test 13 times before passing! After his twelfth attempt, some people recommended (2)*give / giving* up, but his parents encouraged him (3)*to take / take* the test one more time. He got a new instructor, who claimed (4)*have / to have* a 100% success rate. On the day of the test, the instructor (5)*reminded / suggested* Josh to stay calm and forget about the other tests. And it worked! Josh's family organized a big party to congratulate him on finally (6)*pass / passing* the test.

b Finish the sentences so that they mean the same.

1 *We're really sorry we didn't come to the party.*
They apologized...

2 *Would you like to come for dinner, Tom?*
She invited...

3 *Let me help you with that suitcase, Natalie.*
He offered...

4 *Did you eat the rest of that cake, Matt?*
She accused him...

5 VISITORS: DO NOT TOUCH THE ELECTRIC FENCE
The sign warns...

c Think of a conversation or argument you have had recently. Write a summary of what was said.

About a week ago, I argued with my sister. She accused me of...

12.2

a Correct the sentences. Two sentences are already correct.

1 I've never traveled anywhere by **plane**.
2 I have been going abroad **three times in my life**.
3 I'll be studying English for about **seven years now**.
4 At the moment I'm **studying abroad**.
5 By the time I've finished this exercise, I won't have eating for **three hours**.
6 This morning at 7:15 I'd been **taking a shower**.
7 Tonight at 10:00 I'll probably been **having dinner**.

b Rewrite the phrases in bold so the sentences are true for you.

WRITING BANK

4 A MESSAGE BOARD

1 Work in pairs. Answer the questions.

- Do you ever read or post messages on online message boards or forums? When? Why?
- Why do you think people use anonymous names on online forums? How do they choose these names?
- Are people nicer when they post messages online or when they talk face to face? Why?

2 a Work in pairs. Read BigED's posting to the message board. Discuss what you think people will write in reply.

b Read the replies. Did anyone mention your ideas in 2a?

3 a Answer the questions. Who...

1 feels positive about modern society?
2 criticizes another posting?
3 complains about an increase in crime?
4 complains that people are more unfriendly nowadays?
5 claims that young people are disrespectful?

b Whose opinions do you a) agree with? b) disagree with? Why?

4 Complete each sentence with one word from the message board.

1 You shouldn't .... by saying that everyone is rude!
2 I .... agree that salespeople are really rude these days!
3 Your comments about the unemployed are outrageous. You're .... that everyone on benefits is lazy!
4 .... on young people I know, I'd say that teenagers read all the time, mostly online.
5 We don't know if the people on the subway were young or old, but that's .... the point. *No one* helped the pregnant woman!
6 I know graffiti is a crime, but I .... to say that for me it's a kind of art form.

5 a Open a message thread about one of these topics, or about a topic of your choice.

1 The worst thing about working/studying is...
2 The stupidest rule I've come across is...
3 The best movie/book set in my country is...

b Pass your message to the student on your right. Write a reply to the message you receive.

6 a Repeat 5b until each message has six replies. Return the message and replies to the message writer.

b Read the replies to your message. Which is the best? Why? Tell the class.

Comments in chronological order (Total 6 comments)

Is Society Becoming More Antisocial?

BigED

Hi, guys. I thought I'd open up a new thread after my trip to work today. I was on a packed subway, and a pregnant woman got on. I was shocked because no one gave up their seat for her! What I want to know is: is society becoming more antisocial?

JohnStordy

I totally agree that people's behavior is getting worse. People eat fast food and play loud music on public transportation. Teenagers especially are to blame; they have no respect for anyone.

Lola

@JohnStordy I think your comment is really unfair. How can you generalize like that about teenagers? You're also assuming that the subway was full of young people! How do you know that?

Momoftwo

Based on people I know, I think people are *more* socially minded today. A lot of my friends are members of charities, and my kids try to raise money for endangered species. That's not antisocial. People never did things like that in the past.

KC

I think a lot of people here are missing the point. Society is getting worse and worse. You can't put your bag down for one minute these days. There were four burglaries in my town last week. For the same reason, many elderly people are afraid to leave their own homes. My grandmother never locked her front door. Imagine that today!

Ro99

Everyone is talking about bad behavior. But I have to say that for me, the biggest problem is that people don't talk to you. When I go to the mall these days, nobody chats or tries to help you. They're not interested in you as a person. That's antisocial to me.

Done

TIP

Keep your message board posts short. If you want to reply to a specific message, you can use "@" and the poster's name. You can express strong opinions and disagree, but be careful that disagreement doesn't become a personal attack on another poster.

5 A FORMAL E-MAIL

1 Work in pairs. In what situations would you write a formal e-mail?

to apply for a job...

2 a Read Mariko's e-mail and answer the questions.

1 Who is she writing to?
2 Why is she writing to him/her?
3 How does she know him/her?
4 What does she want to know in particular?
5 Why does she want to work on a master's degree?

File Edit View Tools Message Help

Dear Professor de Witt,

1 I am writing to ask for information about the Master's Degree in Sports Psychology at Southern University. I heard about the degree through your colleague Dr. Sourav Baksi at a university visitors' day last month. He advised me to contact you to find out more about the program and in particular the admissions requirements.

2 I am currently completing a four-year degree in biology at Osaka University and would like to move into the area of sports science. While studying here, I have represented Japan in lacrosse in under-21 category and have become very interested in the role of psychology in sports. I would like to work as a psychologist with athletes participating in team sports to improve their performance and team dynamics.

3 In addition to my sports training and academic studies, I am also fluent in English, having passed the CAE exam last year.

4 I would be very grateful if you could tell me whether my degree would be accepted as a relevant qualification for the master's program.

5 I look forward to your reply. Thank you in advance for your help.

Sincerely yours,

Mariko Sato

b Match a–e to paragraphs 1–5.

a asking a specific question
b ending an e-mail
c outlining qualifications and reason for interest in the program
d explaining the reason for writing
e information about additional qualifications

3 Rewrite the informal sentences with formal equivalents from Mariko's e-mail.

1 Is my degree in the right subject for your master's program?
2 Someone you work with, Mike Jones, told me about the degree.
3 Right now, I'm just finishing a BS degree in biology.
4 Can you give me some information about the program?
5 I'll tell you something else, I also speak really good English.
6 Hope to hear from you soon. Thanks for everything!

4 a Think of a course you would like to take. Prepare notes on...

1 your relevant experience.
2 your reasons for wanting to do the course.
3 your qualifications.
4 what you would like to do after the course.

b Write a formal e-mail asking for information about the course. Use some of the phrases from Mariko's e-mail. Follow the paragraph headings in 2b.

5 Exchange e-mails with a partner. Underline any mistakes and return the e-mail to your partner to correct.

TIP

Keep formal e-mails brief and to the point. Organize the different points you want to make logically and separate them into paragraphs. Use formal vocabulary (e.g., *advise*, *currently*) and avoid using contractions.

6 A FOR-AND-AGAINST ESSAY

1 **a** Work in pairs. Look at the images and answer the questions.

1 Where are the people? What are they doing?
2 What are the positive and negative aspects of these different ways of working?

b Read an essay about working from home. Which of your ideas in 1a, question 2, are mentioned?

2 Work in pairs. Read the guidelines for writing a for-and-against essay. Then follow instructions 1–3.

- Spend time thinking about the topic and make a list of points for and against.
- Start each paragraph with a topic sentence that summarizes the content of the paragraph.
- Use phrases to introduce and add arguments.
- Write one paragraph giving the arguments for and one giving the arguments against.
- Don't use opinion words (*I think*, *I believe*, etc.) in the introduction or main body.

1 Underline the topic sentence in each paragraph of the essay below.
2 Underline the phrases used to introduce or add arguments.
3 List the main advantages and disadvantages of telecommuting mentioned in the essay.

3 Are phrases 1–6 used a) to introduce an initial argument, b) to add arguments or c) to conclude?

1 Overall, I believe... ......c......
2 Another negative aspect of... ....
3 First of all... ....
4 To begin with... ....
5 In conclusion... ....
6 One argument in favor of/against... ....

4 **a** Work in pairs. Choose topic 1 or 2. Make a list of points for and against.

1 Does modern technology make life more convenient?
2 Is teamwork a means of success?

b Write your for-and-against essay, using the plan below. Follow the guidelines in 2 and use some of the phrases in 3.

Introduction: Introduce the topic
Main body: Two paragraphs—one with arguments for and one with arguments against
Conclusion: Your opinion or a balanced view of the topic

5 Work in pairs. Exchange essays and answer the questions.

1 Are the arguments for and against convincing?
2 Does the essay follow a clear, logical order?

TIP
Avoid using informal or colloquial language in your essay and try to express your views in an unemotional way. In for-and-against essays, it is very important to balance arguments on both sides.

Telecommuting

Telecommuting, or working from home, is a growing trend nowadays. It is likely to become more popular in the future, bringing changes in work and family life.

The main advantage of telecommuting is that it saves time and money for workers. The time that workers currently spend commuting is reduced or completely cut as they make fewer trips to and from the office. As a result, workers have more time and energy for work. Furthermore, telecommuting saves people money as they spend less on transportation, gasoline and parking. This also benefits the environment by reducing carbon dioxide emissions. An additional advantage for workers is that they have a better balance between work and home life. They can spend more time with their families because they can arrange their work around other commitments, such as taking children to school.

While the idea of more time at home and less time traveling to and from work is attractive, there are some drawbacks to telecommuting. In the first place, people may feel unable to escape their work and may even work longer or more unsocial hours. In addition, the quality of work may suffer because of the reduced face-to-face interaction with other employees. Finally, there is the possibility that managers feel they have less control over what workers are doing.

In my opinion, the trend towards more flexible ways of working can only be a good thing. It may take a while to adapt to a new system, but overall the benefits outweigh the disadvantages.

COMMUNICATION BANK

7.3 Speaking, page 79, Exercise 1a

Student A

You want to organize a competition. The whole department will form teams and take part. Team members have to work with two people they don't know very well. The competition could be anything, e.g., find two English words for every letter of the alphabet. The first team to finish is the winner.

8.1 Speaking, page 85, Exercise 1a

Crime 1

A group of young people had an illegal party in the park last night. They played loud music all night, and there was a lot of shouting and noise. The neighbors were unable to sleep.

Crime 2

A local politician was elected because he promised to address youth crime. Now he has been found guilty of tax evasion, with $700,000 hidden in offshore bank accounts.

Crime 3

A burglar was targeting the homes of elderly people to steal TVs, money and jewelry. He didn't hurt anyone or carry a weapon, but people were terrified when they heard him in their house.

Crime 4

A fight started at a soccer stadium between two rival groups of fans. One fan pushed a rival, who fell from the top row in the stadium. He was seriously injured and is now recovering in the hospital.

8.2 Speaking, page 87, Exercise 1a

Student A

You were visiting a city, admiring the architecture, when a man came toward you waving a piece of string. You were curious, so you stopped to see what he was doing. As soon as you slowed down, he insisted on tying the string around your finger. He started to twist it, making a friendship bracelet. When you tried to walk away, he got angry and asked you to pay for the bracelet. He wouldn't let you go until you had given him $20.

9.0 page 92, Exercise 2a

Student A

Maneki Neko

Maneki neko figures are very popular in Japan and are believed to bring good luck to the owner. *Maneki neko* in Japanese means "beckoning cat." The cat always has one paw raised. Tradition says a raised right paw attracts good luck and money and a raised left paw attracts customers. For this reason, people usually display the figures at the entrance to their home or business.

The Evil Eye

This is a photo of a nazar or "evil eye" bead hanging on someone's front door. These amulets are meant to protect you, your loved ones, your home or business against the "evil eye"—or bad energy. They are very common in Turkey, Greece and parts of the Middle East. They're made of colored glass. You can find them in homes and offices, in jewelry, on cars or taxis, baby clothes and even cell phones.

11.1 Speaking & Reading, page 118, Exercise 2a

Student A

ENGKEY

The kids think their teacher sounds rather robotic today, which is hardly surprising. She's short, white and made of plastic. This is Engkey, the brainchild of Dr. Choi-taek, a government scientist from Korea. Dr. Choi-taek is an expert in robotics, which is increasingly important in his country.

This is reflected by the high cost of one of these machines—at 10,000,000 won (about $9,000) each, Engkey isn't the cheapest teacher around! But the cost is worth it because a robot can go to islands and rural areas, where few native speakers work as English teachers. Once there, it can start immediately—and it has a tough teaching technique the students sometimes don't expect! Engkey is the kind of teacher who doesn't accept errors, and pronunciation mistakes are met with a strict "Not good this time!"

However, there are some drawbacks to using a robot teacher. The main one is that Engkey can only correct mistakes that are already in its database. That's one reason it can't interact with students all the time. Nevertheless, the Koreans are hoping to use more robots like this in the classroom in the future. So perhaps Engkey really does represent the future of classroom teaching.

11.5 Prepare for Task, page 125, Exercise 6

Student A

Read about the item below. Do you think it would be a good gift item?

Description

Purpose:	novelty ice cubes for drinks
Design:	1980s Arcade game character, PacMan
Cost:	$10

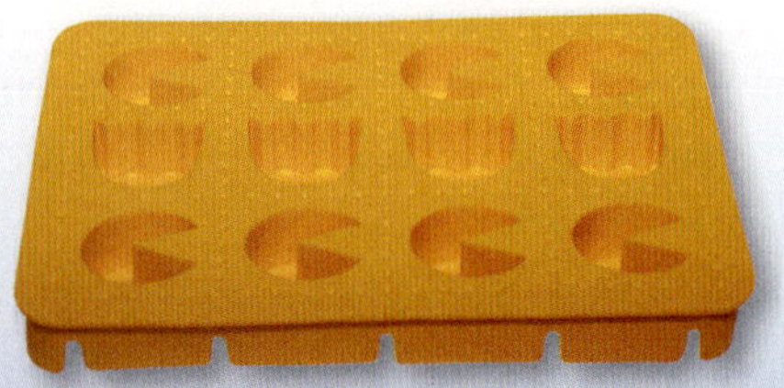

7.3 Speaking, page 79, Exercise 1a

Student B

Get the whole department together in one big room. Invite people to walk around the room and talk to everyone to see if they can find one connection between them. The connection must be something that isn't obvious (not e.g., "We both have blond hair."). The people with the most unusual connection win.

8.2 Speaking, page 87, Exercise 1a

Student B

You were walking your dog in the park when a couple ran out of the bushes saying that a swan had attacked their child. The woman pointed to the lake, where what looked like a baby was floating face down in the water. They were very distressed and said they couldn't swim. You took off your jacket and ran into the water. But when you got to the baby, you realized it wasn't real—it was just a doll! You looked around, and the couple were taking your phone and money out of your jacket. They took $70 and your cell phone, which was very expensive.

9.0 page 92, Exercise 2a

Student B

Lucky Pigs

In Germany it is believed that pigs bring good fortune, financial prosperity and health. This dates back to hard times in the past when you were considered lucky if you had a pig to feed your family and survive the winter. People often make pigs out of marzipan and give them to friends between Christmas and New Year to bring good luck for the coming year.

Lucky Bulls

Not many people have heard of lucky bulls. But in the south of Peru, you often see pairs of terracotta bulls on the rooftops of houses. The bulls are considered to be symbols of luck and fertility for the whole household. The bull figures are often accompanied by a cross and a bunch of flowers.

11.5 Prepare for Task, page 125, Exercise 6

Student B

Read about the item below. Do you think it would be a good gift item?

Description

Purpose:	keeps you dry in the rain
Design:	made from potatoes. Recycle it by planting it in the ground!
Cost:	$20

11.1 Speaking & Reading, page 118, Exercise 2a

Student B

WATERBOXX

Many areas of the world receive very little rainfall, which makes growing trees a real challenge. To solve this, Pietr Hoff has come up with an intriguing innovation called the Waterboxx. It's basically a bucket that has a cover with two holes in it to catch rainwater. In the center is an opening to plant a tree.

It enables plants to grow and survive in areas where there is little water, like the Sahara, which is one of the driest regions on earth. It is a breakthrough that could bring salvation to enormous numbers of people worldwide. Mr. Hoff believes that the Waterboxx could help replant many of the world's forests that have been destroyed by heavy industry over recent years.

The good news is that Mr. Hoff, whose previous job was exporting flowers, has recently received a grant from the government in his native Holland. This means that he doesn't need to make a lot of money from his invention. So the price for the Waterboxx could be as low as $1 (although it is now $199 for ten). Mr. Hoff's simple idea could soon change the lives of millions of people and make him an inspiration for future inventors.

REVIEW D, Vocabulary, page 136, Exercise 2a

Student B

Imagine this is your store. Follow the instructions on page 136.

7.3 Speaking, page 79, Exercise 1a

Student C

You want to set up an anonymous bulletin board at the entrance to the office. Everyone can write a message and put it on the board without their name. They can write about anything related to work, especially things that make them happy or unhappy about working on a team. At the end, people choose the best two messages.

11.5 Prepare for Task, page 125, Exercise 6

Student C

Read about the item below. Do you think it would be a good gift item?

Description

Purpose: alarm clock
Design: top flies off to wake you up
Cost: $20

9.0 page 92, Exercise 2a

Student C

Ladybugs

Ladybugs are considered lucky in almost all cultures. In particular, it is thought to be bad luck to kill a ladybug. The superstition might have evolved as a way to protect ladybugs because they eat many pests that destroy farmers' crops. It is widely believed that if you see a ladybug, or if one lands on you, you will have good fortune.

Elephants

Asian elephants are regarded as symbols of good fortune in Thailand, where they are a national symbol. They represent loyalty, wisdom, elegance and a long life. Some people even pay to walk under an elephant three times because they believe this will bring them good luck. Statues of elephants are found in many temples. People often rub their head for luck.

10.3 Speaking, page 113, Exercise 1b

Unemployment

In 2011, unemployment became a serious problem in the Republic of Ireland, and many young people left the country to find work. But Feilim Mac An Iomaire didn't want to emigrate. So to find work he advertised himself on a giant billboard in Dublin. It worked—he received several invitations to job interviews from interested companies.

7.3 Speaking, page 79, Exercise 1a

Student D

You want to organize a dinner for the whole department, but instead of going to a restaurant, you are going to hold it in the office cafeteria. Everyone has to prepare a dish, and they must cook it themselves (they cannot buy one). All the dishes are placed on the table anonymously, and people have to guess who cooked each one. Then everyone sits down to enjoy the meal together.

7.1, p. 72, Ex 2a

Speaker 1

Oh, I read about this story in the newspaper... This woman tried to go shopping in her pajamas, but the supermarket staff told her that her clothes were unacceptable! It was very funny, really. She must have felt very foolish. The supermarket said that it wasn't illegal or immoral to shop in pajamas, they were just worried that allowing people to shop dressed like that might offend some customers. I think their decision was fair... I mean, dress codes in the USA are generally pretty flexible, but you have to draw the line somewhere! Otherwise people will just become more and more careless about things like this.

Speaker 2

We made a big mistake when we were on vacation in the Dominican Republic. We wanted to visit the famous Higuey Basilica, one of the most noteworthy cathedrals in Latin America. Unfortunately, the man at the door refused to let us in. He wasn't impolite or anything, but he explained that we were dressed inappropriately. We both had shorts on, and I had bare shoulders. Although they can give you a scarf to cover your shoulders, we couldn't cover our legs so we weren't allowed to go in. I was really disappointed. According to my guidebook it was OK to wear shorts anywhere in the country. It turned out to be full of inaccurate information, really kind of useless. I'll get a more reliable one next time.

Speaker 3

Last year, I was on vacation in Thailand. On my first day, I went to visit a Buddhist temple. The woman at the gate was really helpful, but just as I was about to go in, she asked me politely to take my shoes off. Wearing shoes in a Buddhist temple is considered disrespectful. I was a little embarrassed because I'm always really careful when I go abroad and read up on local customs and dress codes, things like that. I think it's irresponsible to arrive somewhere without doing any research. Anyway, my shoes were expensive, but I didn't worry about leaving them outside. I know there are dishonest people around, but most of the people I met while traveling were very trustworthy.

7.4, p. 80, Ex 2a

A: Good afternoon, Helpline, how can I help you?

B: Oh, finally, a human being! My flight's been delayed, but no one has given us any information. I want to know what's going on.

A: I'll do my best to help you, sir. I'm afraid a lot of our flights have been delayed today due to bad weather.

B: Yes, I can see it's due to bad weather. But the problem is, no one's telling us anything. There are enormous lines at all the information desks.

A: That's to be expected in this situation, sir. You need to wait for further announcements.

B: Look, I know it's not your fault, but this is really frustrating!

Flight AA234 to Chicago has been canceled due to poor weather conditions.

B: Oh great! First they said the flight was delayed, and now they're saying it's canceled.

A: I'm very sorry to hear that sir.

B: I'm waiting here with my wife and kids. What are we supposed to do now?

A: You should be able to book another flight online.

B: Book another flight online? Do you have any idea how difficult that is? I looked on my iPad, and there are no flights available for the next two days!

A: I'm very sorry sir, but that is the present situation regarding flights.

B: Well, I'm afraid that just isn't good enough! You need to add more flights! We don't live here. We're on vacation. All I'm asking for is a flight home.

A: If you are unable to fly, you should be able to get vouchers for a hotel for tonight.

B: Oh I see. We can get vouchers for a hotel, can we? We stay there for free? How do we go about that?

A: If you go to the information desk, you can get the vouchers.

B: And the hotel provides dinner?

A: Yes, the voucher covers the cost of your meal.

B: That's something, I suppose. But I really think you should have better plans in place. This isn't the first time it's happened.

A: I'm sorry, but that's the best we can do. The weather has surprised everyone.

B: Yes, I understand that. Thank you.

7.5, p. 80, Sounding frustrated

1 Oh, finally, a human being!
2 Yes, I can see it's due to bad weather.
3 First they said the flight was delayed, and now they're saying it's canceled!
4 Do you have any idea how difficult that is?
5 That's something, I suppose.

8.4, p. 88, Ex 1

Today a very real courtroom drama is playing out before our eyes. Sixteen-year-old Marvin Duthie is sitting in the dock at the county courthouse. He has been charged with vandalism and attempt to damage public property.
This morning Marvin's head hung low as his mother testified in the witness box. Her face was pale and her voice trembled. She didn't dare catch Marvin's eye because they both knew that if she had not contacted the police, Marvin wouldn't be on trial here today.

Marvin had been having trouble at school. When his favorite teacher and mentor, Mr. Glasby, took early retirement and left the school, things got worse. Who knows, if Mr. Glasby had stayed on another year, Marvin might still be in school instead of in a courtroom. Marvin got involved with a gang at school. He started hanging out with his new friends and spraying graffiti around the town. When his mother found out, she tried to talk to him, but he just laughed at her. She wasn't happy with the situation, but she wasn't too worried either—after all, there are much worse crimes than painting graffiti. And if Marvin and his friends had stuck to graffiti, things might not have turned out so badly. But soon painting illicit messages on trains and railroad property lost its excitement. The boys had moved on to something new, something much more dangerous.

Mrs. Duthie told the court how she had started checking the messages on Marvin's phone and how she found out that the boys had been vandalizing the local railroad tracks. She was terrified. Not only was Marvin putting his own life in danger by wandering onto the tracks, but the damage they had caused could have resulted in a catastrophic accident. If a train had been derailed, Marvin and his friends could have been responsible for multiple deaths and injuries. She phoned the police in a panic and did something no mother ever wants to do: she reported her son. The police investigated and found some damaged tracks and a screwdriver with Marvin's fingerprints on it.

When Marvin was arrested, his grandmother claimed that he had been with her all day when the crime was committed. If it wasn't so common for family members to lie to protect each other, the police might have believed her, but her evidence was confused and contradictory. Marvin was put on trial along with three of his friends.

Today Marvin pleaded guilty and said that he truly regretted what he had done. The court has heard all the witnesses, including his former mentor, Mr. Glasby, and the jury is currently considering its verdict. Marvin could receive a fine of up to $1,000 or even be sent to a reform school or juvenile detention center. But as it is his first offense, he is more likely to be sentenced to community service and given a second chance.

9.4, p. 98, Ex 2

A: In our podcast last month we had a discussion about youth unemployment. This month's podcast topic isn't quite as serious as the last one. Today we'll discuss working in the television and movie industry. Most people think this profession is impossible to get into unless you have the right family or connections. "Good luck with that," your friends say with a smirk when you tell them of your intentions. "It's not what you know, it's who you know." So how much of an advantage do the right contacts give you in this industry?

B: Well, it's certainly very competitive and jobs are always scarce. An important factor is having relevant industry experience. However, it's very difficult to find paid work experience. In addition, television and movie companies are usually in capital cities, where living costs are far higher than in other parts of the country. Bear in mind that you may have to work without pay for a year or more to get work experience... so who's going to pay your bills in the meantime? Wealthy parents might come in handy here.

A: But it's not the only way, surely? You could always take out a bank loan if you're running low on cash, or work part-time for pay?

B: Yes, of course, but it's slightly easier if your family or friends help you. And to continue, how do you get that important work experience placement in the first place? Creative industries are nowhere near as open as other professions. You need contacts. If you have a relative in the industry and you want a job, they'll take care of it for you.

A: But surely training is just as important as contacts? My cousin works in Bollywood in India. I lost touch with him for a while, but I got an e-mail last week saying he just got a job as an assistant director. He didn't have any industry contacts. He went to film school and got the right training.

B: But that's not the norm in Bollywood. He must have had a lucky break. The Indian movie industry runs along similar lines—it's about who you know more than your skills. Bollywood isn't any less competitive than Hollywood, and even talented people have a lot of trouble getting into the industry. And your cousin still had an advantage that many don't—he went to film school. How do you know the right college to go to and how to apply? I bet he went to a good school, so it was easier to get into college.

A: Yes, I think he did... So it all comes back to having the right connections?

B: Well, not always. There are plenty of examples of rags-to-riches stories, too. For example, in 1945, a photographer was taking pictures at a factory, when he caught sight of one of the workers. Her job was to spray plane parts and inspect parachutes. The photographer thought she had a very interesting look and encouraged her to contact a modeling agency. She took his advice. She got rid of her factory job and became a very successful model, which eventually led to a career as a movie actress. She changed her screen name to Marilyn Monroe.

A: From factory worker to star of the silver screen—talk about a lucky break!

B: Yes, luck can play an important part, too, though you might not become quite as famous as Marilyn Monroe!

9.8, *p. 101, Ex 2a*

Today I am going to discuss the question: How much does luck contribute to success in life? Let me start by saying that luck does play an important role in life. There's "big-scale" luck such as being born into a wealthy family or winning the lottery. But there's also "small-scale" luck, such as a chance encounter with an influential person. In this talk I'm going to argue that success in life is not limited to luck. While there's little we can do to influence big-scale luck, it's ultimately our attitude and behavior that influence small-scale luck.

In my opinion, there are three main factors that influence our success in life. The first of these is being open to new ideas and experiences. Lucky people regularly expose themselves to new experiences and environments and build and maintain diverse networks. They are more likely to create, notice and act upon chance opportunities in life. Because of this, more opportunities come their way.

Another important point is that lucky people have a more positive outlook on life. Positive people can deal with setbacks and challenges better than negative or pessimistic people. They don't give up at the first obstacle and continue to persevere in the face of failure. They also expect their good luck to continue in the future, and because of this, they take more calculated risks in life.

My final point is that lucky people are able to change bad luck into good fortune by learning from past experiences. They change how they behave to reduce the chances of bad luck in the future. It's important to remember that lucky people are more likely to view a disaster as an opportunity for learning and growth, whereas unlucky people in the same situation would complain and blame someone or something else.

In conclusion, luck can affect us positively or negatively in life. However, in most cases there are other factors that are far more important in making a success of life.

10.1, *p. 106, Ex 2a*

A: The credit crunch is on. Everything is expensive and for many families, it's hard to get by. This is a time when people should be cutting back on their spending... and yet the stores are full of customers. More people are taking out loans, even though some will take years to pay off their debts. Retail expert Terry Landry explains why people keep shopping during a financial crisis.

B: The stores are very good at using retail psychology. They use tricks to manipulate customers into spending money. For example, imagine you've been saving up for months to buy a new bed. In the store you see feather pillows and attractive, colorful duvets next to it. So displaying similar items together tempts people to buy them. And if you're forking out hundreds of dollars for a bed, buying a pillow and a duvet as well doesn't seem too expensive.

A: I see!

B: Store layout is very important. One big computer store created their display with lots of empty space and just a few products, with no price labels, on big pine tables. This gives the impression that a store has a few, high quality products, and the space makes customers feel more comfortable and confident by giving them better access to the products.

A: And so, because there are no prices displayed, you don't know if the store is ripping you off until you get really interested in a product?

B: Absolutely. Layout is important for supermarkets, too. Fruit and vegetables look fresher in natural light, so they are almost always at the front. Fish and meat are in a section with white walls and aluminum tables as they look fresher in clean, white light. Supermarkets also know that men usually just grab what they need in a store and leave. Major items are placed in the middle of the aisles, and men's products are placed at the back of the store. That way they have to walk past other things to get to what they need and may buy on the way.

A: So you go to the supermarket because you've run out of shaving cream and come out with cereal, cookies and detergent? Are there techniques for women, too?

B: Well, for example, younger women are more likely to buy clothes if they're in disorderly piles. It suggests that they are popular. If piles are too neat, it gives the impression that no one is buying the clothes. I once sold hundreds of silk scarves just by leaving them in disorderly piles in my store.

A: And what about color?

B: Yes, this can influence us to choose a product. Purple is associated with luxury, so supermarkets often use purple cardboard packaging to sell a premium brand, for example, a more expensive ready-prepared meal.

A: Thanks, Terry, I never realized how much I was being manipulated...

10.2, p. 108, Ex 2b

A = Announcer, **I** = Interviewer,
C = Christopher

A: And now we join Emma Grigson in the studio, for this week's edition of *The World Today*.

I: Good morning and welcome to *The World Today!* Now, a round red rubber ball for my dog. A set of shiny steel table knives. A huge pine writing desk. What do they have in common? Well, I bought all of them this week, and they were all made in either China or Taiwan. And here to talk about China's remarkable economic success is Christopher Yu of the Chinese Chamber of Commerce here in New York. Christopher, welcome to the program!

C: Thank you, Emma, it's a pleasure to be here.

I: So, Christopher, why is China growing so fast?

C: Well, Emma, for a variety of reasons. First, today's China now has the capacity to make very up-to-date, sophisticated products. For example, just think about the magnificent curving steel lines of the Bird's Nest Stadium, the National Stadium in Beijing.

I: Mmm, yes, it's an amazing piece of architecture.

C: Yes, well as you know, it was built for the 2008 Olympic Games, and I think it's a great example of China's recent success. The government is very anxious to encourage innovation, and there are plenty of creative people with new ideas and ambition, for example, the Chinese designer of the National Stadium, Li Xinggang. But the stadium is also an example of how we're open to developing projects with foreign companies—it was a joint venture with a leading Swiss engineering firm. This kind of collaboration creates more jobs and brings the Chinese economy in closer contact with international markets.

I: Hmm, that's really interesting. So foreign companies are attracted to China because it's such a creative environment.

C: Well, yes, partly, but another factor in China's growth is its growing productivity. People often work longer hours than in the West, and, of course, we have a very large population. At one stage, there were 17,000 people working on the Bird's Nest Stadium. Neither a U.S. nor a European company could employ that many people at the same time.

I: Wow, 17,000 people! That's incredible! So, it looks as if China's economy has really started to take off in the twenty-first century.

C: Well actually we mustn't think that Chinese growth is a purely modern phenomenon. Look at the Great Wall of China! In many ways it's a similar achievement to the Bird's Nest Stadium. It was a hugely ambitious project, and there was nothing else like it at the time. And you know, China has always been the workshop of the world, at the forefront of new technology. Paper, gunpowder and printing were all invented there. And for hundreds of years, China was the center of the world's silk industry.

I: So, it's all looking very positive for the next few decades.

C: Absolutely! But there's just one problem. I can't think of a single world-famous Chinese brand, can you? Lenovo is a major computer maker in China, and Ningbo Bird is one of its biggest cell phone makers. But neither Lenovo nor Ningbo Bird has global recognition.

I: So why do you think that is?

C: Well, I think to a large extent it's because most Chinese companies are either owned by foreign companies or just make parts of other products. So you might see a U.S. company's name on that big square cardboard box for your computer, but it was probably made in China.

11.1, p. 116, Ex 2a

I came across this new gadget on the Internet the other day. I think it's quite a breakthrough—for someone like me at least, who doesn't know how to type! It's a great alternative to the conventional Qwerty keyboard, called the "fast finger" keyboard. It's different from a traditional keyboard because the letters are arranged in alphabetical order to make typing easier. It's especially good for kids who are first learning to write. Such a simple idea but so effective! Qwerty boards are so difficult to learn on! I mean, why on earth are the keys in that order? For those of you who don't know, a traditional keyboard is called a "Qwerty" keyboard because of the letters on the first six keys on the board: Q-W-E-R-T-Y. Ever wondered why the keys are arranged in this unnatural order? Early typewriters, it seems, were originally designed with the letters in alphabetical order—far more logical. But there was a drawback: designers noticed that the keys kept jamming, kept getting stuck, because people were typing too fast. So they had to figure out a way to slow typists down to stop the keys from jamming. And that's how they came up with the Qwerty keyboard. They rearranged the letters in an unfamiliar order. This slowed typists down and caused fewer jams. Of course, over time, typewriter technology improved, but keyboards stayed the same. Until now that is, when someone came up with the idea of the fast fingers alphabetical keyboard. The inventor of the new keyboard got this flash of inspiration after watching a mechanic typing information on a computer in a repair shop. He spent ages looking for the right letters on the keyboard and had a long line of frustrated customers waiting to be served. If only the keys were arranged alphabetically, she thought. A friend of the inventor also noticed how we use the same abbreviations over and over again on the computer, especially for e-mailing, chatting and instant messaging. So this unusual keyboard also has special keys for common abbreviations such as ASAP, FYI and LOL. So far it has not been a commercial success, mainly due to the fact that the vast majority of keyboards are Qwerty boards and you can't really avoid using them. But early adopters say that once you get used to it, it really does make typing much easier. So, just another gimmick, or a great innovation that will radically change the way we type? What do you think?

11.8, p. 125, Ex 3a

A: Hey, Monica, can you come here a second?

B: What is it?

A: Well, I'm thinking of buying an e-reader, but I'm not sure which one. I've been looking at some online. You know a lot about these kinds of things. Could you give me some advice?

B: Of course. So this is the first one?

A: Yeah, it's called the Skiff.

B: OK... I think it's designed for reading newspapers and magazines mainly.

A: I know – I mostly read newspapers anyway. What do you think of it?

B: Well, on the one hand, it's larger than other e-readers, so it isn't so convenient to carry around. But on the other hand it's incredibly light and thin and has the highest resolution display. It's also designed to be more durable than other e-readers, I think!

A: That sounds good. And what do you think of the Kindle?

B: It's really popular, I know lots of people who have them now. It's reasonably priced, and the battery lasts up to a month! One thing to bear in mind, though, is that you can only buy Kindle e-books through Amazon, you know, to upload on it.

A: That's OK, I use Amazon a lot.

B: But since you read newspapers more than books, maybe the Skiff is a better option? Though you should also consider the iPad... Of all the options, it has the greatest functionality. You can do almost anything with it.

A: And it has a touch-sensitive screen, while the Kindle uses buttons.

B: But on the downside, it costs a lot more than the others. Another thing in favor of the Skiff is that it's flexible; I mean, you can actually bend it. I really like that idea.

A: They all seem to have their pros and cons. I guess I need to think about it a little more.

B: Oh Colin, you can never make up your mind!

12.1, *p. 126, Ex 3a*

Speaker 1

I went on this incredible trip to the Canary Islands in the Atlantic Ocean. We were on a ship named the *Lord Nelson*. It was like an old pirate ship or something, really massive. We weren't just passengers, we were sailing the ship—it was a once in a lifetime experience. There's this one memory that really stands out to me... an incredible memory. I was on night watch, it must have been about 3 a.m.—and we were all up at the helm—you know, at the back of the ship where you sail the ship from, with the wheel and compass and everything. We were sailing past Tenerife, one of the big islands, and suddenly there were lots of little fishing boats all around us, right across our path. It was kind of weird, there were we on this amazing ocean voyage on this huge ship, and at the same time there were all these little fishing boats just going about their business, getting on with their day-to-day life. Our job was to keep a course but at the same time to look out for these little boats, so we didn't hit any, and it was the dead of night, so you had to look really hard. Anyway, um, I was at the helm when the first mate, who's the captain's assistant, said that everyone else had to go to the front of the ship to correct a sail that wasn't right, so all the other people in my team and the first mate went off to pull on some ropes and things. So there I am, sailing this huge ship with all its sails above me, the island to my left and the clouds all lit up by the moon... totally stunning... all I can hear is the waves and the wind, and I'm the only person there! It feels like I'm totally alone. Honestly, it was awesome. I'll never forget that...

Speaker 2

I was traveling in India a few years ago, and one day I decided to visit the beach temples in Mahabalipuram. The temples are over 5,000 years old and stand on the shore of the Bay of Bengal, facing due East. I wandered down to the beach, and there were the temples... simple, stone temples. The setting was so fantastic that I decided to get up early the next morning and go down to watch the sun come up over the bay and over the temples. I got up early, at about 5 o'clock, had a cup of wonderful sweet chai from a street vendor and walked toward the beach. The day was just about to break. There were strings of purple and pink in the sky—absolutely breathtaking. I'd been expecting to be alone... to be one of the only people down on the beach at that time, but when I got there I just couldn't believe my eyes... there were crowds and crowds of people down on the beach, hundreds of people silhouetted against the ocean and the purple-pink sky. Then I remembered, they were pilgrims, mainly young people, I had heard about them. They were on a one-month pilgrimage, visiting various sites, and one of the things they had to do was bathe in the waters of Mahabalipuram at sunrise. But still, seeing them all walking together into the ocean, fully dressed, their clothes soaked by the waves, was truly awe-inspiring!

Speaker 3

I was taking an English course in Canada—we were sitting in class one morning... in January I think it was... and suddenly I noticed the teacher. She turned to look out the window, and a smile spread across her face. So we all looked. It was snowing! Big, heavy, slow snowflakes were floating past the window. I stopped and stared, it just took my breath away! I had never seen snow before. There were a few of us in the class, another Guatemalan and a couple of students from Brazil, who'd never seen snow either. We must have looked so funny, all staring out the window in amazement! She walked to the door, and we followed her out onto the street, into the snow. It was incredible, so different, so strange, so beautiful... Almost overwhelming. I swear I just stood there like a child with my face turned up and my hands held out, catching snowflakes on my tongue. My classmates laughed at me, and then we started a huge snowball fight. We all got completely soaked—and freezing! It really was amazing, unforgettable... I wish I'd had my camera! This photo was one I took later, toward the end of the day, we were walking home along the river... it all looked absolutely spectacular.

R21, *p. 138, Ex 1a*

D = Darren, **M** = Michael, **K** = Katy

M: I just don't understand it. There were $80 in the cupboard earlier; there're only $35 now.
D: Hey! Don't look at me. I haven't touched the money.
M: Nobody else could have taken it, Darren. You're the only one who knew where it was.
D: I didn't! I swear! I mean, I wasn't even here most of the day. Maybe you, I don't know, took it for shopping or something and forgot.
M: Don't be ridiculous! I wouldn't forget something like that.
D: Look, Dad, I have to go out now. The game starts in half an hour, and Katy's picking me up.
M: You haven't heard the last of this!

K: You won! At last! Congratulations, Darren, it was a great game.
D: Yeah, I know, it was getting a little embarrassing with all those defeats. Thanks for the lift, Katy.
K: No problem. Anyway, how about we go for a drink to celebrate?
D: Sure. Or, we could go to Tino's for pizza if you like?
K: Oh, I don't think I can. I don't have much money until next week.
D: That's all right, it's on me.
K: But I thought you were broke, too.
D: Nah, it's OK. My dad lent me some money.
K: But you bought the gasoline the other day and the coffees yesterday...
D: Don't worry about it, I'd like to. Please let me buy you lunch. My thank-you for, you know, getting me here on time.
K: Well, if you're sure... But I'm getting it next time, promise.
D: Great! Come on, then. Let's go!

R22, *p. 138, Ex 1a*

Hi, Susan, how's it going?
...
You'll never guess what's happened!
...
Darren and Katie went out for lunch together on Saturday...
...
Yeah, honestly! Amalia saw them in Tino's.
...
They went out after the game to celebrate his team winning, or something.
...
Well, they went for pizza, and he paid for the meal...
...
Yeah, but wait... it gets better. Apparently he stole the money from his dad!
...
He did! I can't believe it either. And now his dad won't let him go out for a whole month!
...
Well, not really, he only has himself to blame. It was a pretty stupid thing to do.

Contents

American Big Picture

B2 [Upper Intermediate] Split Edition b

Workbook

Alastair Lane

Richmond

www.americanbigpicture.net

Richmond

58 St Aldates
Oxford
OX1 1ST
United Kingdom

Printed in Mexico

First edition: October 2012

Av. Río Mixcoac No. 274, Col. Acacias,
Del. Benito Juárez, C.P. 03240, México, D.F.

Publisher: Deborah Tricker
Content Development: Eleanor Clements, Sarah Thorpe
Editor: Emily Binner
Audio Production: Motivation Sound Studios

Cover Design: Pentacor Book Design, Lorna Heaslip
Design & Layout: Lorna Heaslip, Dave Kuzmicki
Picture Editor: Helen Reilly/Arnos Design Ltd
Art Coordinator: Dave Kuzmicki
Illustrators: Francis Blake c/o Three-in-a-Box Ltd., page 24; Myles Talbot, page 73; Ron Wilson, page 29

Photos:
Arnos Design Ltd/David Oakley; Erden Eruc; Guardian News & Media Ltd 2011; Penguin Books Ltd; Maria Sanclement,; South West News Service/ Blake Ezra Cole/MASONS; TouchTunes Interactive Networks. ALAMY/Gunter Marx/EV, Big Cheese Photo LLC, Tomas de Arno, Jef Maion, Yu Liang Wong, Richard Levine, Jonathan Pearson, Chris Wilson, Photos12, Apex News and Pictures Agency, Ria Novosti, Outdoor-Archiv, Allesalltag, SHOUT, AF Archive, Fancy, Chuck Franklin, Ed Bock/Corbis Flirt, ITAR-ITASS Photo Agency, incamerastock, Catherine Paffey, TongRo Image Stock, The Art Archive, Steve Hamblin, Alamy Celebrity, Image Media Partners Ltd/Impact Photos, Sornos Images; CORDON PRESS; CORBIS/Hiep Vu/First Light, Matthew Wakem, Aurora Photos, Mallet/ Photocuisine, David Trilling, Image Source, Rainer Holz; FOTOLIA/ biker3, Antonio Oquias, Sergent, Misha, Paul Fleet; GETTY IMAGES Tom Kitchen, Tao Associates, Yellow Dog Productions, David Malan, Digital Vision, Frank Siteman, Jenifer Thermes, Alexander Nemeneov, Jupiter Images, Gary Yeowell, Photographer's Choice, Mark Lewis, Juice Images, Lounge Park, 2004 CBS Photo Archive, Simon Bruty, Adam Pretty, Lanny Ziering, Gray Mortimore, Photodisc, Bellurget Jean Louis, Amama Images, Stocktrek Images; GETTY IMAGES SALES SPAIN/Thinkstock; ISTOCKPHOTO/nkbimages, mattjeacock, Franco di Meo, denituvel, fonikum; PA PHOTOS/David Longstreath, Jose Acosta; ISTOCKPHOTO/ Getty Images Sales Spain; REUTERS/Attila Cser; REX FEATURES LTD/ Tom Campbell/Splashdown Direct, Lyndon Mechielsen/Newspix; THINKSTOCK/Istockphoto, George Doyle, Dynamic Graphics, Polka Dot, David de Lossy, Hemera, Creatas, Zoonar, Bananastock, Photos.com, Comstock; Albert Velasco; ARCHIVO SANTILLANA. © THINKSTOCK: Ablestock.com p. 9.

Cover Photo:
Big Apple at sunset, Fotolia © dell #9950038

We would like to thank the following reviewers for their valuable feedback which has made *American Big Picture* possible. We extend our thanks to the many teachers and students not mentioned here.

(Argentina): Cecilia Chiacchio, Ingrid Suhring; (Brazil): Ana Falcao, Virginia Garcia, Patricia McKay, Cynthia Phillipps, Bia Sousa; (Colombia): Kathleen Canal; (Italy): Morgan Cox, Karen Geiger, Sarah Stats; (Mexico): Emma Dominguez, Melissa Ferrin, Lupita Neve, Coral Ibarra Yunez; (Poland): Malgosia Adams, Marta Rosinska; (Spain): Vicki Anderson, Juan Carlos Araujo, Karen Dyer, Gabby Maguire, Fiona McClelland, Karin Rickatson, Almudena Verdugo Valcarce, Andy Walsh; (UK): Cathy Ellis, Howard Smith, Jonathan Stoddart

The Publisher has made every effort to trace the owner of copyright material; however, the Publisher will correct any involuntary omission at the earliest opportunity.

This book was printed in los talleres de Editorial Impresora Apolo, S.A. de C.V. Centeno 150-6, Col. Granjas Esmeralda,C.P. 09810, México, D.F. in december 2012

TRANSCRIPT	CONTENT	TRACK
7.1	Page 43, Exercise 5	15
7.2	Page 46, Listening, Exercises 2 & 3	16
8.1	Page 49, Exercise 6	17
8.2	Page 52, Functional Language, Exercises 1 & 2	18
8.3	Page 52, Listening, Exercise 1	19
9.1	Page 55, Exercise 5	20
9.2	Page 58, Listening, Exercise 1	21
T3	Page 61, Progress Test 3, Listening	22
10.1	Page 63, Exercise 8	23
10.2	Page 66, Listening, Exercise 1	24
10.3	Page 66, Listening, Exercise 2	25
11.1	Page 69, Exercise 5	26
11.2	Page 72, Listening, Exercises 1 & 2	27
12.1	Page 75, Exercise 7	28
12.2	Page 78, Listening, Exercises 1 & 2	29
T4	Page 81, Progress Test 4, Listening	30

7 SOCIETY AND YOU

VOCABULARY

Rules & behavior

1 Complete the words in the conversation.

A What does that sign say?

B It says that it's (1)i __ l __ g __ l to release animals into the river.

A Why would someone do that?

B Lots of people get the wrong pet. They buy a baby turtle, for example, and they don't realize that it's a completely (2)__ __ ap __ __ op __ __ __ te pet for a city apartment. It soon grows very large, and they don't have the space for it, so they put it in a river. It's really (3)i __ r __ __ p __ ns __ b __ e.

A But putting it into the river doesn't do any harm, does it?

B Yes, it does! The animal could destroy the entire habitat. Dumping pets in the river is completely (4)u __ a __ c __ __ t __ b __ __. People should find other homes for them instead. It's really (5)u __ r __ as __ n __ b __ e to think that a pet will be able to survive in the wild.

A That's true. I know my aunt's cat wouldn't survive a minute without her!

2 Complete the sentences with the correct form of the words in parentheses.

1 You shouldn't use your credit card on that website. It doesn't look very ____________ . (trust)
2 This GPS is ____________ ! It can't find any of the addresses I need! (use)
3 If you can be ____________ , you can often get cheaper flights by changing the day you leave or arrive. (flex)
4 Jimmy was being really ____________ when he said he wouldn't obey the dress code. (child)
5 Do you know a ____________ builder? We need someone to redo our kitchen. (rely)
6 I'm always very ____________ when I wash these glasses because I don't want to break them. (care)

Bureaucracy

3 Complete the sentences with the correct phrases from the box.

birth certificate enrollment form formal complaint form job application passport application proof of address tax return

1 Your ____________ shows when and where you were born and who your parents are.
2 If you want to open a bank account, you have to provide ____________ to show where you live.
3 I was very unhappy with the service I received, so I asked for a ____________ .
4 It can take a long time to fill out a ____________ because there are usually a lot of questions about your work experience.
5 To find out how much money you owe the government, you need to fill out a ____________ .
6 When I started at the college, I had to fill out an ____________ .
7 I need to complete this ____________ because I have to go abroad later this year.

Collective nouns

4 Which words from the box can you use to describe 1–7?

crew flock gang herd horde mob pack swarm

1 A large group of pigeons ____________
2 A large group of people protesting violently in the street ____________ , ____________
3 A group of children or teenagers who spend time together ____________
4 An enormous number of mosquitoes flying together ____________
5 A group of wolves or wild dogs ____________
6 The people who work together on a plane ____________
7 A group of buffalo ____________

Vocabulary Extension

Further prefixes

5 **a** Read the definitions. Then complete the words in 1–5. Use the same prefix for both a and b.

inter-	between two things
mis-	wrongly, badly
over-	too much, more than usual
re-	again, repeated
under-	not enough, less than usual

1 a Our team was _______confident. We thought it would be easy to win the football game, so we didn't play hard enough and we lost!
  b Your vacation plans are completely _______ambitious. You can't travel all around Mexico in a week!

2 a The suffix *-ful* is frequently _______ spelled "f-u-l-l."
  b He was often _______understood because he didn't communicate very clearly and he was very shy.

3 a The store wouldn't sell my cousin the DVD because it was for over-18s and she was _______age.
  b The vegetables are a little _______done. Let's put them back in the oven for twenty minutes.

4 a Synonyms are words that are _______changeable. They mean the same thing.
  b We're going on an _______continental flight between the U.S. and Brazil.

5 a These are the _______designed business cards. Do you like them better than the original ones?
  b Those jam jars are _______usable, so don't throw them away. I'll use them when I make my own jam.

b 7.1 Listen and check.

6 Complete the sentences with words from **5a**.

1 The ____________ website is much easier to use than the old one, and it looks better, too.
2 My name was ____________ on my boarding pass, so they wouldn't let me on the plane.
3 It's important that we have ____________ products for all our cell phones. If a gadget works with one phone, it should work with all of them.
4 Kerry failed his driving test because he was ____________ and didn't prepare enough for it.
5 This steak is really ____________ ; it's red! I can't eat that!
6 Most plastic bags are ____________ , so I don't know why we throw so many away.
7 There are lots of ____________ airlines operating between Amsterdam and destinations in Asia.
8 The government has these really ____________ plans. They won't be able to do everything in just five years!
9 Frederick is writing a book, but nobody likes it. He doesn't care because he thinks he's a ____________ artist and that people will recognize his talent in the future!
10 They wouldn't let us into the nightclub because they thought we were ____________ —and we didn't have our ID cards!

Bring It Together

7 Complete the posts with words from the box. There are two words that you don't need.

careful disrespectful flexible flock helpful ID card illegal intercontinental gang overconfident passport application unacceptable

Niko: When I moved here, I needed to get a(n) (1) ______________ because it's (2) ______________ to live here without one. I waited at the office for nearly three hours, which I thought was completely (3) ______________ . Finally I got the form, and someone told me how to fill it out and was really (4) ______________ . Has anyone else had an experience like this?

Brendan: Once when I was on vacation, I was walking down a busy street when a (5) ______________ of men suddenly surrounded me, and one of them stole my passport. It was awful because I wasn't expecting it. I think I was (6) ______________ . I had heard stories about this kind of thing but I didn't think it would happen to me. I went to the Irish Embassy, and they were really nice and helped me fill out a(n) (7) ______________ so I was able to go on with my vacation.

Min: Last year, I moved from Vietnam to the States. It was a(n) (8) ______________ flight, and we could only take 25 kilograms of luggage. I was really (9) ______________ when I packed my bags, but they were still 30 kilograms. Luckily, the man at the check-in desk said he would be (10) ______________ with the rules for me because I was going to live in the U.S. I thought that was really kind of him.

GRAMMAR

Past modals: *Should have/could have*

1 **a** Put the words in the correct order to make sentences.

1 your you should you passport have with

____

2 for a asked formal could have complaint you form

____

3 fined having they a for him car have could dirty

____

4 shorts worn have temple to shouldn't I visit the

____

5 if she photos Iris was to should have allowed take asked

____

6 we problem have could a

____

b Which sentences in **1a** are in

1 the present? ______________

2 the past? ______________

2 Complete the conversations with the correct form of the words in parentheses.

1 A I didn't get the job.
B Well, you ______________ more time on your application. You did it too quickly. (should/spend)

2 A That man was driving much too fast! This is a busy street!
B I know! He ______________ someone. (could/hurt)

3 A I've just discovered my passport's expired!
B Oh no! We ______________ the expiration date before we booked our flights. (should/check)

4 A They wouldn't let me in the cathedral because I was wearing shorts.
B Oh dear! I ______________ you they don't allow you in if you're in shorts. I went there last year. (could/tell)

5 A I can't believe the airport staff charged me $40 for excess baggage!
B Well, you ______________ so much luggage. You'll never wear all those clothes in two weeks! (should/bring)

6 A Did you finally finish filling out your tax return?
B Yes, finally! Thank you so much. I ______________ it without your help. (could/finish)

3 Correct the sentences. Mark (✓) one correct sentence.

1 You should have check the form before you sent it in.

2 We should changed our clothes before we went to visit the temple.

3 You shouldn't have downloaded that movie.

4 You couldn't went to work yesterday; you were too sick.

5 We could park in front of the station, but we parked in the parking lot instead.

6 Anton should have driven as much as possible next week to prepare for his driving test.

Past modals: Speculation & deduction

4 **a** Look at the photo and responses 1–4. What do you think the man looking for?

1 Are you sure you packed it? You **might have left** it at home.

2 Oh no, it **must have fallen** out of your bag!

3 You **couldn't have lost** it. I saw you put it in your bag after we went through passport control.

4 Check your bag again. You **might not have looked** carefully.

b Look at the words in bold in responses 1–4. Match them to uses a–d.

a a speculation about something we are sure happened __________

b a speculation about something we think happened __________

c a speculation about something we think didn't happen __________

d a speculation about something we are sure didn't happen __________

5 Rewrite the sentences using the words in bold. Keep the same meaning.

1 I'm sure they liked my job application because I have an interview next week. **must**

They must have liked my job application because I have an interview next week.

2 I don't believe that Lucas went to Chile. **couldn't**

____

3 I think my job application got lost in the mail because I haven't received a reply. **must**

____

4 Maybe Jack didn't know about the dress code. **have**

____

5 His visa application was rejected. It's possible that he made a mistake on the form. **might**

____

6 Perhaps Mika didn't read your e-mail. **may**

____

6 Which responses are correct? Mark (✓) the correct box: a, b or both a and b.

1 I heard about this strange new chewing gum on the radio, and I think it was from Singapore.

a It must have been from Singapore because chewing gum is illegal there.

b It couldn't have been from Singapore because chewing gum is illegal there.

a ☐ b ☐ both a and b ☐

2 Do you know who put that sign up yesterday?

a It could have been Dino because he's responsible for safety here.

b It couldn't have been Dino because he's on vacation this week.

a ☐ b ☐ both a and b ☐

3 His application for an ID card has been turned down.

a Really? He might have filled out the form incorrectly.

b Really? He must have filled out the form incorrectly.

a ☐ b ☐ both a and b ☐

4 I have a photo of you driving a purple car, but I can't remember what year it was taken.

a It must have been 1988 because I borrowed my mom's purple car that summer.

b It couldn't have been 1987 because I didn't get my driver's license until 1988.

a ☐ b ☐ both a and b ☐

5 I spoke to someone at the front desk yesterday. A tall man with a mustache.

a Ah! That must have been Gerhard. It sounds like him.

b That might have been Gerhard because he has a mustache.

a ☐ b ☐ both a and b ☐

Bring It Together

7 Complete the text with the correct form of the words in parentheses.

The Year of the Locust

As thousands of locusts descended on homes and villages in Senegal, Morocco, Mauritania and Egypt in 2004, people (1)________ (must/be) terrified. Experts estimate that the swarm (2)________ (may/be) the size of London and the swarm (3)________ (might/include) up to 50 million insects. The only good news is that the locusts (4)________ (could/cause) much more damage by entering the main food-producing areas of the countries. Fortunately, despite their "swarm intelligence," they (5)________ (couldn't/know) about the location of the main corn-producing fields of Senegal, or they would have devastated these areas. That (6)________ (could/create) a huge food crisis across the continent.

As for how the swarm happened, scientists believe that good rains had created plenty of food for the locusts, and this (7)________ (must/lead) to the sudden explosion in their numbers. Some people think that scientists (8)________ (should/predict) the swarm, but others say that it was just a natural phenomenon. Either way, the swarm made 2004 "the year of the locust" for the victims of this terrifying plague.

FUNCTIONAL LANGUAGE
Criticizing

1 Complete the words.

A Hello. City Water Service.

B Hello. I contacted your department weeks ago about a problem with water coming into our house. Since then, nobody has done anything. I want to know what's (1)g__________ on! My reference code is A91-0R.

A Mr.... Jackson. I have a record of calls from you on June 16 and 21.

B That's right. The last time, a lady said you would look into it. But the problem is, no one is telling us (2)a__________! Have you any (3)i__________ how much damage has been done to my house?

A Well, we have arranged for someone to visit you within the next three weeks.

B Three weeks! I'm afraid that just isn't good (4)e__________! The water is damaging my house now! All I'm asking (5)f__________ is someone to come and look at it.

A And they will come, within three weeks.

B So what are we (6)s__________ to do now? Nothing? Three weeks is too long. You should have better systems in (7)p__________. I've had problems with the city water services in the past. This isn't the (8)f__________ time this has happened. I'd like to speak to your Complaints Department, please.

B I'll put you through to Complaints now, Mr. Jackson. Hold the line, please.

LISTENING
Inferring relationships

1 Look at the words for addressing people. Are they formal (F) or informal (I)?

1 darling F / I ______
2 dear F / I ______
3 ma'am F / I ______
4 officer F / I ______
5 sir F / I ______

2 **a** 7.2 Listen to four short conversations. Number the words in **1** in the order you hear them. There is one word that you don't need.

b Match conversations 1–4 to photos a–d.

3 Listen again. In which conversation (1–4)...

1 has the speaker not understood something? ______
2 is the speaker trying to get to work? ______
3 has the speaker had this problem before? ______
4 does the speaker want to complain about something? ______

STRATEGY When you listen to a conversation, think about the relationship between the speakers. Are they speaking formally or informally? How do they address each other? Making logical deductions about how the speakers know each other can help you understand what they are saying.

READING Skimming

1 **a** Look at the text. What kind of text is it? ______________________

b Read the text quickly. Who are the people 1–4? Match them to the words from the box.

a fictional character	a journalist	a lawyer	a parent

1 Gian Ettore Gassani ____________ 3 Friday ____________
2 Mara O ____________ 4 Alain Elkann ____________

2 Read the text again more slowly. Answer the questions.

Parents Ordered to Change Child's Name from Friday

By Chris Irvine

Italy's Court of Appeal has banned a couple from naming their son Venerdi (Friday) because the name could expose the boy to ridicule. Named after the manservant of Daniel Defoe's famous novel *Robinson Crusoe*, the Cassation Court said the name was associated with being a servant. The judges also ordered the boy to be renamed Gregorio, named after the saint's day on which he was born.

The boy's parents, known only as Mara O and Roberto G, had said they should be free to name him as they pleased and said they would continue to call the boy Friday, describing it as "nice." They even threatened to call their next child Mercoledi (Wednesday).

The verdict provoked mixed reaction across Italy. Gian Ettore Gassani of the Italian Association of Matrimonial Lawyers agreed with the ruling. He told an Italian news agency that Italian law mandated changes "when the child's name is likely to limit social interaction and create insecurity."

Italian journalist Alain Elkann argued that Friday was a good name, adding: "It would have been different if they'd called him Friday the 13th."

Friday joins an ever-growing list of banned names, which are becoming more popular arguably due to the celebrity trend of giving unusual names to their children.

In February, a judge in New Zealand made a young girl a ward of the court so she could change her name from Talula Does The Hula From Hawaii. The judge said the name embarrassed the nine-year-old and could expose her to teasing.

Other names banned include twins called Fish and Chips, although Number 16 Bus Shelter was one of the more bizarre ones allowed. In New Zealand again, last year a couple was banned from naming their baby 4Real, so they settled on Superman.

According to genealogy website findmypast.com, the UK has six boys named Gandalf, 29 Gazzas and even 36 Arsenals.

1 Why did the court reject the name Friday?
____

2 What name did Venerdi's parents say they would use for their child now?
____

3 What name does a journalist suggest is worse than Friday?
____

4 Why are more and more people giving their children unusual names?
____

5 Where else have unusual names been banned?
____

6 Which unusual names have been permitted?
____

STRATEGY When you read a difficult text for the first time, don't panic! Don't worry about understanding every word. Instead, read the text quickly and try to get a general understanding of it (the gist). Look for facts that will tell you the main subject of the text. Then read the text again more slowly.

8 CRIME AND PUNISHMENT

VOCABULARY

Crime

1 Read the descriptions. Write the name of the crimes.

1 The supermarket says that thousands of razors are stolen from their shelves every year. ____________
2 Five people were almost killed when a car bomb was left near the police station. Police believe it was the work of a violent political group. ____________
3 They stopped an elderly man while he was walking in the park. They showed him their knives and told him to give them all his money. ____________
4 Someone went into our house while we were on vacation and stole the TV. ____________
5 Some teenagers set fire to a school in their neighborhood. ____________
6 In the novel that I'm reading, a rich businessman is shot by a rival while he is sleeping. ____________
7 Some kids broke all those windows for fun. ____________
8 They received a note yesterday saying their 21-year-old son had been captured and would not be released unless they paid a ransom of $2 million. ____________

2 Complete the text with the words and phrases from the box. There is one that you don't need.

capital punishment community service corporal fine in prison prison sentence

Do Existing Punishments Fit Today's Crimes?

The most serious penalty for a crime is (1)____________, the death penalty. In many countries, this is not a legal punishment and life (2)____________ is given instead for crimes like murder. However, despite its name, this may only mean a (3)____________ of 30 years. The reason is obvious. Too many people are in jail, and it's expensive to keep them there. That's why governments prefer to tell people to pay a (4)____________ for minor offenses like speeding and why younger criminals can just be warned not to commit the offense again. Another punishment is (5)____________, where criminals have to work for free in their local area. Some people believe that these punishments are not serious enough and that (6)____________ punishment would be more effective because physical pain has more impact on people. Making the punishment fit the crime is a challenging issue faced by governments around the world. What do you think? Tell us your opinion by adding your comments below.

3 Choose the correct options to complete the sentences.

1 Someone's stolen my *apartment / sneakers*!
2 My boss has been charged with *$10,000 / tax evasion*.
3 A boy at my school got arrested for *arson / some money*.
4 Don't do that! You're committing *a fine / a crime*!
5 Last week a man robbed my *cell phone / parents' house*.
6 The company was found guilty of *illegal file sharing / life in prison*.

Scams

4 Complete the words.

A Have you ever been a victim of crime, Helmut?

B Well, yes. It was a scam really, not a big crime. I was on vacation, and I wanted to rent a quad bike. The man asked for my ID card as security. I was a little (1)n _ ï _ _ really because I trusted him.

A I suppose if you're a normal, (2)l _ _ -ab _ _ i _ g citizen, you do trust people.

B Yes, exactly. When I returned the bike, the man said it was damaged and that he wouldn't give me back my ID card unless I paid a fine! We had a big argument, and then this policeman appeared. Although I think he was a (3)b _ g _ _ one because he didn't listen to me at all. I couldn't be sure if he was real or not, but I wasn't going to argue with an (4)a _ th _ _ i _ y f _ _ u _ e like that. I just paid, and the man got an extra $100.

A So the man renting quad bikes and the policeman were both (5)c _ _ a _ t _ _ ts? Poor you. Well, put it down to experience. You won't be (6)t _ _ en _ n like that again.

On trial

5 Read the clues. Complete the crossword with words for the law.

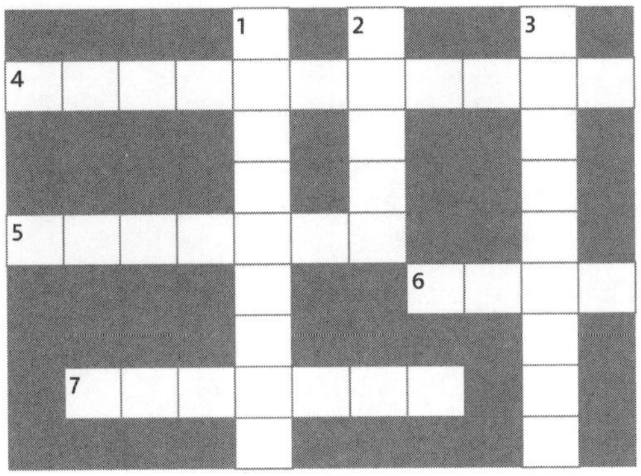

Across

4 The ... accuses someone of a crime.
5 The ... speaks for the person who is accused.
6 The ... is made up of members of the public. They watch the trial and decide if the person is guilty or not.
7 A ... is someone who saw the crime and who tells the court what he/she saw.

Down

1 The ... is the person on trial. He/she has been accused of something.
2 The ... supervises the trial and makes the final decision about what punishment to give.
3 The ... is where the trial takes place.

VOCABULARY EXTENSION Police work

6 a Read the words and their definitions. Then complete the sentences with the words.

alibi *(n)* a piece of information that proves you did not do a crime because you were somewhere else
bail *(n)* before a trial, you can pay this money to the court to be free and not in prison
convicted *(adj)* found guilty of a crime by a court
DNA testing *(n)* a way of looking at someone's genetic code (DNA), e.g., from blood, to identify them
handcuffs *(n)* metal rings that the police put around someone's wrists when they arrest them
suspect *(n)* someone that the police think might have committed a crime

1 The police identified the murderer using ____________ .
2 The judge has set your ____________ at $10,000 so you can be free while you are waiting for your trial.
3 After the bank robbery, the police arrested one man, who they believe is the main ____________ .
4 Gordon's ____________ is perfect. The robbery happened at 5 p.m., when he was on a plane over the Pacific.
5 The police put ____________ on the mayor when they arrested him for corruption.
6 The thief was caught by the police, ____________ of robbery and sent to jail.

b 8.1 Listen and check.

BRING IT TOGETHER

7 Complete the text with the words from the box. There is one word that you don't need.

bail capital commit guilty judge jury murder prosecution suspect testing witness

The CSI Effect

The TV show *CSI New York* is so successful that it's having an impact on real-life trials in the courtroom. This is called "the CSI effect." Many crimes can be solved based on normal evidence: if a (1)______ saw the defendant (2)______ the crime, for example. However, in the USA, the twelve-person (3)______ now expects to see forensic evidence as well. This is particularly true where the verdict could be (4)______ punishment.

The problem is that when experts on *CSI* use DNA (5)______ , on blood and hair, for example, they say that it is completely trustworthy. When they investigate a crime, the TV characters quickly identify a (6)______ by saying that his DNA matches DNA on the victim. But in real life, when people accuse someone of a crime such as (7)______ , the experts can only say DNA evidence could match. Their information is not really 100% accurate. However, today, people are suspicious of a case if it doesn't contain this type of evidence. It's difficult to believe someone is (8)______ of a crime without seeing the same forensic evidence as on TV. Often, the (9)______ says this is unnecessary. Nevertheless, the (10)______ still have to provide this evidence because that's what the people on the jury expect!

GRAMMAR

If sentences: Imagined situations (1)

1 Complete the text with the correct form of the verb in parentheses.

Luke Hartigan's crime blog... Police lineups

If the police (1)____________ (suspect) you of a crime, one thing they would use to test your identity is a police lineup. If real life were like TV, everyone in the lineup (2)____________ (look) more or less the same. But, in fact, they often look completely different! This is not a big problem. If the police (3)____________ (put) the real criminal in the lineup, they would be identified correctly, after all. Or would they?

In fact, police lineups are often used to test witnesses. If a police officer (4)____________ (not/trust) a particular witness, they would show them two lineups, the first one without the suspect. They (5)____________ (only/show) them a second lineup if the witness didn't wrongly identify a suspect in the first one.

If the police only showed an untrustworthy witness one lineup, he or she (6)____________ (just/choose) anyone. This is because a bad witness thinks the real suspect must be there! If a witness (7)____________ (make) a false identification like this, an innocent person's life could be ruined. That is why the police need to control what happens in a lineup very carefully.

2 Correct the sentences. Mark (✓) two correct sentences.

1 If you were in the store yesterday, would you have stopped the robbery?
2 If the criminals had go to prison, they wouldn't have committed any more crimes.
3 You might not have gotten that virus last week if you hadn't downloaded things from that file-sharing site.
4 There hadn't been so much crime last year if there had been more police officers on the street.
5 If the jury saw this evidence in last year's trial, they could have found the man guilty of murder.
6 If there had been a lot of vandalism in the old days, everyone would have tried to stop it.
7 I was mugged! If I didn't hide my credit card in my sock, they would have taken that, too!
8 If the flight hadn't been delayed, they would arrive five hours ago.

Wishes & regrets

3 a Order the words to make sentences.

a the wish dishes would wash the I he
____
b would put online they wish I the lyrics
____
c the Sunday opened only drugstore on if
____
d knew drive to how if I only
____
e wish work I have I didn't to
____
f started classes if the only later
____

b Match 1–6 to responses a–f in **3a**.

1 You can't take this course because you have soccer practice at the same time. ______
2 Marco doesn't do much housework, does he? ______
3 There's no public transportation to the festival, so we can't get there. ______
4 I really can't understand the words of this song. ______
5 It's a shame you can't come to the beach with us. ______
6 I have a terrible headache, but I can't find any aspirin. ______

4 Choose the correct options to complete the conversations.

1 A Rick got caught shoplifting at the local store.
B Oh no! If only he *didn't become / hadn't become* friendly with the wrong crowd!

2 A Someone has vandalized my car again!
B If only we *had found out / could find out* who keeps doing it!

3 A I wish we *hadn't gone / could go* on that walk.
B I know. I can't believe that woman accused us of trespassing!

4 A The police have said that Internet crime is rising all the time.
B If only they *had monitored / could monitor* everyone's computer to catch the thieves.

5 A Veronica's been accused of tax evasion.
B I know. She told me that she wishes she *had filled / filled* out her tax return more carefully.

If sentences: Imagined situations (2), mixed time frames

5 Which sentences are correct? Mark (✓) the correct box: a, b or both a and b.

1 a If they had found the burglar guilty, they would have sent him to prison yesterday.
b If they had found the burglar guilty, he would be in prison today.
a ☐ b ☐ both a and b ☐

2 a If the woman had gone to prison, she wouldn't be doing community service now.
b If the woman had gone to prison, she wouldn't have done community service now.
a ☐ b ☐ both a and b ☐

3 a If I hadn't bought a paper yesterday, I wouldn't find out about the trial.
b If I hadn't bought a paper yesterday, I wouldn't have found out about the trial.
a ☐ b ☐ both a and b ☐

4 a We would still have capital punishment if the government hadn't changed the law in the 1960s.
b We would still have had capital punishment if the government hadn't changed the law in the 1960s.
a ☐ b ☐ both a and b ☐

5 a If they had caught the robber, he would be at the police station by now.
b If they had caught the robber, he would have been at the police station by now.
a ☐ b ☐ both a and b ☐

6 a You wouldn't have lost your money if you hadn't left your bag open.
b You would have some money now if you hadn't left your bag open.
a ☐ b ☐ both a and b ☐

7 a If last night's fire was caused by arson, there might still be evidence there.
b If last night's fire had been caused by arson, there might still be evidence there.
a ☐ b ☐ both a and b ☐

6 Rewrite the sentences, using the words in bold. Keep the same meaning.

1 I'm feeling sick, so I didn't go to work this morning. **if/weren't**
If I weren't feeling sick, I would have gone to work this morning.

2 Yolanda didn't get the job so she's still working at the same company. **if/wouldn't**
____

3 You don't watch TV, so you didn't see the news about the kidnapping yesterday. **if/have**
____

4 I didn't cover up my PIN number. That's why the thief now has all my money. **if/had**
____

5 Monica missed the bus, so she's walking home. **if/wouldn't**
____

6 They parked their car in the wrong place and now they have a parking ticket. **if/wouldn't**
____

7 He visited the doctor. That's the reason why he's in the hospital now. **hadn't/might**
____

8 We put security cameras in the store so shoplifting isn't a big problem for us now. **if/be**
____

Bring It Together

7 Complete the text with the correct form of the word(s) in parentheses.

Miscarriage of Justice

In the past, in Britain, criminals could be executed by hanging. This ended after a terrible miscarriage of justice.

Back in 1950, Timothy Evans was executed for the murder of his daughter after a very short trial. If the trial had been longer and more thorough, Evans (1) ____________ (not/die) because in 1953 the police learned that another person living at Evans's house had murdered other people. If the jury (2) ____________ (not/find) Evans guilty, the police might have stopped the real killer earlier.

We all wish the police (3) ____________ (be) perfect. However, mistakes like this still happen today. Take the case of Norwegian Åge Vidar Fjell. In 1990 he was found guilty of murdering his neighbor. Twenty years later, the courts declared him innocent because of his mental state. Even if he (4) ____________ (be) at the crime scene, he could not have shot the victim. If only the court (5) ____________ (accept) this medical evidence back in 1990! Fortunately, Fjell was able to enjoy his freedom again. If Norway (6) ____________ (have) the death penalty in 1990, he and other wrongly convicted people (7) ____________ (not/be) alive today.

Many of us wish that things like DNA testing (8) ____________ (provide) definite proof of someone's guilt. However, there are still problems, and for this reason, among others, the death penalty remains illegal in many countries.

FUNCTIONAL LANGUAGE
Changing the subject

1 8.2 Listen to three conversations. Mark (✓) the topics that are mentioned.

arson burglary court dinner fraud graffiti judge meeting money vandalism

2 a Complete the sentences from the conversations in **1**.

1 No, sorry. ____________ way, have you heard that she's leaving?
2 Next week apparently. ____________ reminds me, she borrowed some money from me last week. I should get it back before she goes.
3 ____________, if you do see her, can you remind her that we're going out for dinner this evening?
4 ____________ trials, did you see the report about vandalism on the news last night?
5 ____________ I forget, can you come in a little early tomorrow? We have a lot to cover.
6 All right. I'll try to be here by eight. ____________ the subject, have you heard if there's a date for the arson court case?
7 ____________, I should go. I don't want to miss my train.

b Listen again and check.

LISTENING
Listening for detail

1 a 8.3 Read Ben's notes about his trip. Listen to an announcement and answer the questions.

Catch the 9:35 train from Baltimore to New York.
Arrive in New York 11:10.
Change in New York for 11:45 train to Boston.
Arrive Boston 12:40.

1 How will Ben travel to New York now?
____
2 What time will he leave?
____
3 What time will he arrive in New York?
____
4 How does this affect his trip to Boston?
____

b Listen again. Correct six mistakes in the text below.

Ladies and gentlemen, may I have your attention please? Due to looting on the railway line, trains will not be running from Miami to New York this morning. Passengers for the 9:35 service to New York should wait in the ticket office for the replacement bus service. The buses will depart at about 10:15 and should arrive in New York at about 12:00. Trains from Baltimore to Trenton are also affected. Please see signs in the station for more information. I'm very sorry for this change in our services, but the problem was only discovered this morning by the station staff. We hope that all services will be back to normal by early evening.

STRATEGY When you listen to a difficult audio, don't panic if you don't understand every word. Try to stay focused and listen for the key information you need.

WRITING A story

Things That Go Bump in the Night

(1) It all happened when I was about 14 years old. My parents had gone out to an important dinner, and it was the first time that I had spent an evening home alone. It was raining hard, and it was very windy, too, and I remember that I felt really scared as I lay in bed. Eventually, I dropped off to sleep.

(2) Suddenly, I woke up. There was a strange noise downstairs! Silently, I lay in bed, listening. At first, I thought it was my parents coming home, but the clock said it was midnight, and I knew they wouldn't be back until two. Nevertheless, there was a steady tap, tap, tap. I was not alone!

(3) "It must be burglars," I thought. My heart was beating fast and I didn't know what to do. Even if I waited in bed, they might come upstairs. I needed to call for help, but there were no cell phones in those days, and I needed to go to the living room to get to the phone. Slowly, I got up and I started to creep downstairs.

(4) The rain had stopped, and the moon was shining through the windows. In its light, I saw a shadow on the kitchen floor. It had four legs and a tail moving from side to side. It did not look human. Happily, I ran downstairs towards the trespasser. It was a cat!

(5) Although we didn't have any pets, the kitchen door had a cat flap put in by the previous owners. The cat had gotten in, but then it couldn't get out. So it was trapped, and it had to hit the flap with its paw to try to escape. That explained the noise. The poor animal was scared, so I quickly opened the door and it ran out into the night.

(6) The next morning when I told my parents about our visitor, we all thought it was very funny, but it didn't feel like that at the time!

1 **a** Read the story quickly and answer the questions.

1 Why was the author by himself?
2 What sound did he hear?
3 Why did he get out of bed?
4 How had the weather changed?
5 How did he solve the problem?
6 How did his emotions about the incident change?

b Find words in the story that mean

1 fell asleep (*paragraph 1*).
2 regular, repeated (*paragraph 2*).
3 to move slowly and quietly (*paragraph 3*).
4 someone who has entered private property without permission (*paragraph 4*).
5 a special door to let a cat come in and out of a house (*paragraph 5*).
6 the foot of a cat, dog or similar animal (*paragraph 5*).

2 Complete the adverbs. Then check your answers in the text.

1 I felt really scared as I lay in bed. E _ _ _ tu _ _ ly, I dropped off to sleep.
2 S _ _ d _ _ ly, I woke up. There was a strange noise downstairs!
3 S _ l _ _ tly, I lay in bed, listening.
4 S _ _ _ ly, I got up and I started to creep downstairs.
5 H _ _ p _ _ y, I ran downstairs towards the trespasser.
6 The poor animal was scared so I q _ _ c _ _ y opened the door...

3 Write a story that ends with one of the sentences below.

1 It's a day that I'll remember my whole life.
2 That's how I met my best friend.
3 It was the best photo that I have ever taken.
4 I was absolutely furious!

STRATEGY When you write a story:

- begin with a phrase like *Once*, *One day* or *It all happened when* to set the scene, e.g., *It all happened when I was traveling around Japan.*
- use the past continuous to describe what was happening when your story begins, e.g., your work, the weather.
- use a range of vocabulary to make your story interesting. Remember to use adverbs, e.g., *suddenly, amazingly, strangely* to describe *how* actions happened.

9 LUCK AND FORTUNE

VOCABULARY

Luck

1 Put the letters in parentheses in the correct order to make words.

1 Some people believe in ____________(stydine)—that our future lives can only happen one way. But I believe ____________(sussecc) or ____________(afeluri) depends on how hard you work.

2 On New Year's Eve in Italy, some people serve lentils to represent ____________(sopiprerty) because lentils look like coins.

3 My partner and I met in the supermarket by ____________(cachen). I think it was ______(tefa); we were meant to be together!

4 People say that health, ____________(ehlawt) and happiness are the key to a good life, but I think health and happiness are much more important than money!

5 Last year I had the good ____________(nutfero) to be offered a new job. I've never been happier!

2 Complete the phrases with *luck*.

1 I hoped I'd win the card game but n __ s __ __ __ l __ __ __ . Erik beat me again!

2 I have to do a big presentation at work tomorrow—w __ __ __ me l __ __ __ !

3 OK, you can go to the party, but don't p __ __ __ y __ __ __ l __ __ __ . Make sure you're home by midnight.

4 I left my scarf on the train, but w __ __ __ a __ __ l __ __ __ , someone will have turned it in to the lost and found office.

5 All my exams went well except for the last one. I guess I had r __ __ o __ __ of l __ __ __ .

6 I just found $10 inside this library book—what a s __ __ __ __ __ o __ l __ __ __ !

Sport

3 Match 1–7 to a–g.

1 We wanted to go running today, but
2 Shelia has lost her racket, but
3 Helen has some knee pads for ice hockey, but
4 To join the baseball team, everyone needs a helmet and
5 We had great seats for the soccer game—
6 There's a lot of chlorine in the pool, so
7 I don't own any golf clubs—

a it's probably next to the court where she last used it.
b we sat right next to the field!
c the track's closed.
d I rent them when I'm at the course.
e it's best to wear goggles and a cap.
f their own bat.
g she needs to borrow some skates to play.

Verb collocations

4 Choose the correct options to complete the conversations.

1 A I'm running *down / low* on cash.
B There's an ATM around the corner. You can get some money there.

2 A We're arranging a conference, and we need to find hotel rooms for fifty guests!
B Don't worry, I'll *make / take* care of it for you. I know lots of hotels.

3 A This washing machine is useless! It never works like it's supposed to.
B Why don't you *get / have* rid of it and buy a new one?

4 A I'll be late home this evening.
B Well, bear in *head / mind* that your grandparents are coming over tonight. They want to see you, too.

5 A Did you have a good time in India? Did you see any tigers?
B Yes, we caught *sight / view* of one for a moment, but then it disappeared into the jungle. They're very shy, really.

6 A Do you have Jeremy's phone number?
B No, I don't. I've kind of *lost / missed* touch with him.

Vocabulary Extension
Sport collocations

5 **a** Match sport collocations a–h to photos 1–8.

a break a record b blow the whistle c hit a shot d make a tackle
e send out (a player) f toss a coin g take a penalty h warm up

b 9.1 Listen and check.

6 Complete the two e-mails with the correct form of the collocations from **5a**.

Hi Ned
The soccer game last night was a disaster! It was 0–0 after 60 minutes. A player on the other team was running toward our goal and I (1)______ and took the ball away from him. The next thing I knew, the referee (2)______ and stopped the game. He penalized our team. He showed me a red card and (3)______ me ______. Because the foul was in our goal area, the other team was allowed to (4)______, so of course it won the game 6–0. It was so unfair!
Aston

Hey Barry
You won't believe the golf game we had yesterday. I was (5)______ before going to play because I have a bad leg. While I was doing that, this new guy at the club asked me if I wanted to play with him. We (6)______ to see who would start, and it was me. So I (7)______ my first ______ ... and the ball went in the hole! A hole in one! My first ever. We couldn't believe it! Then I just played brilliantly and I (8)______ the course ______. No one has ever gotten a better score than me. It was amazing—such a lucky day!
Jack

Done

Bring It Together

7 Put the letters in parentheses in the correct order to complete the text.

In most jobs, (1)__________ (*cussces*) doesn't come from luck, but sports are different. Hitting a lucky (2)__________ (*host*) in tennis or making a last-minute (3)__________ (*ketlac*) in football could mean the difference between winning and losing. This means that athletes the world over are fond of carrying lucky charms to ensure their good (4)__________ (*tournef*). One of the most famous was basketball player, Michael Jordan, who always wore his lucky college shorts underneath his team shorts! He did this for every NBA game he played, hoping they would bring him a (5)__________ (*oktrse*) of luck that would win the game.

Scientists in Germany wanted to find out whether using lucky charms could really change your (6)__________ (*sdytnei*). They gave golfers a "lucky" ball and a normal ball. All the players used the same (7)__________ (*bulcs*), but they all played better with the lucky ball. The scientists' explanation is that when people believe in lucky symbols, it gives them confidence. When athletes are confident, they play better and have a better (8)__________ (*echanc*) of becoming winners. So this really works!

Michael Jordan is a classic example. His lucky shorts helped him avoid bad luck on the basketball (9)__________ (*cruto*). He (10)__________ (*rekbo*) the record for the highest season average score and became one of the most successful players in history.

GRAMMAR

Adding emphasis: Cleft sentences with *is*

1 Complete the words to make cleft sentences.

Morning rituals

Jackie OK everyone. Today's question is: "What's your morning ritual like?" For example, (1)w_________ I love to do i_________ read the paper on my way to work. Most people don't enjoy commuting, but I find it kind of relaxing.

Anwar The (2)t_________ t_________ I always do is drink a cup of strong, black coffee. That's a ritual here in Jordan! The (3)p_________ w_________ I buy it from is a friend of mine, so we always have a chat, too (normally about soccer!).

Letícia I live in Rio and every morning I go for a run at 6 a.m. The (4)r_________ w_________ I go so early is that it's nice and cool at that time of day. Also, there aren't many people out—(5)i_________ the peace and quiet t_________ really clear my head.

Bruce The first (6)t_________ I do in the morning is go to bed! I'm a security guard, and I work night shifts. But before I go to sleep, I always have a meal with my kids: they eat breakfast, but for me it's more like an evening meal!

2 a Complete the second sentence so that it means the same as the first sentence.

1 I chose this profession because I love performing.
The reason why _______________

2 Making people laugh is the best thing about this job.
What I really love about this job
____

3 I also like traveling to different places with the show.
Another thing _______________

4 I don't like my costume. It's not very comfortable.
The thing _______________

5 Seeing my friends in the audience makes me feel anxious.
It's _______________

6 Strangely, my girlfriend makes me the most nervous!
Strangely, the person _______________

b Look at photos a–c. Which job does the person in **2a** do?

a

b

c

Making comparisons

3 Choose the correct options to complete the sentences.

1 That was the *more / most* difficult tennis match I've ever played!
2 Some athletes believe that training *hard and harder / harder and harder* will guarantee success.
3 The *fast / faster* you drive, the quicker we'll arrive.
4 I think she is the *best / better* swimmer I've ever trained.
5 The harder you train, the *more successful / most successful* you will be.
6 Tickets for sporting events are becoming *more and more / more and most* expensive.

4 Complete the sentences with the correct form of the words in parentheses. You may need to add extra words.

1 Emmanuel is ______ athlete we've ever had in this school. (good)
2 Our swimming team is terrible—and we're getting ______ and ______ all the time! (bad)
3 That was ______ football game I've ever seen! Our team was awful! (disappointing)
4 ______ I spend in the gym, ______ I get! (long, hungry)
5 I only started playing golf two months ago. But I'm feeling ______ and ______ each time I play. (confident)
6 Brendon is ______ baseball fan I've ever met; he never misses a game! (dedicated)
7 ______ you skate, ______ it becomes. You really must wear a helmet. (fast, dangerous)
8 ______ I've ever run is twelve kilometers. I was exhausted afterward! (far)

Modifying comparisons

5 Complete the words in the online interview.

Today's online chat is with competitions guru Mia Leung. Join us live from 12:00 EST.

I Mia, you've won over 200 competitions. How?

M It's not that I'm a (1)l __ __ luckier than other people, but I do have some strategies for people who want to become a (2)l __ __ __ __ __ better at winning competitions.

I Tell us more.

M If you enter lots of competitions, you are (3)f __ __ more likely to win something. And don't forget competitions by local businesses. Sometimes only a few people enter them so your chance of winning is (4)m __ __ __ higher than in other competitions. You're (5)n __ __ __ __ __ __ __ near as likely to win a national competition—especially one for a big prize.

I OK.

M In national competitions, you often have to answer a question in 25 words. The competition judges see hundreds of sentences, so if your one is funny, you have a (6)s __ __ __ __ __ __ __ __ better chance of winning. If you can't think of anything funny, then make your entry rhyme. That's (7)j __ __ __ as good as a joke because the judges can remember it.

I Any other advice?

M Yes. Sometimes you can enter many times. I once won a vacation trip like that. It's not (8)n __ __ __ __ __ as difficult as you think!

6 Rewrite the sentences using the words in bold. Keep the same meaning.

1 Playing soccer is easier than playing golf. **not / nearly**
Playing soccer is not nearly as hard as playing golf.

2 Golf clubs and tennis rackets are equally expensive. **just / expensive**
____

3 Watching golf is not nearly as interesting as watching track and field. **nowhere / interesting**
____

4 My new helmet is slightly bigger than my old one. **not / quite**
____

5 Yellow golf balls are as easy to see as white ones. **any / easier**
____

6 Volleyball isn't nearly as popular as soccer. **far / more**
____

7 Our seats in the stadium aren't quite as good as yours. **little / worse**
____

8 The other players on the team are a little stronger than we are. **quite / as**
____

9 My racket was cheap, but it wasn't as cheap as my mom's. **slightly / mine**
____

BRING IT TOGETHER

7 Choose the correct options to complete the text.

The End of Records?

The long jump competition in the 1991 World Championships in Tokyo was the (1)*greater / greatest* competition I've ever seen. The thing (2)*that / what* made it special was the rivalry between Carl Lewis and Mike Powell. These athletes were (3)*slightly / far* better than all the others in the competition. No one else could jump (4)*near / nearly* as far as them. Lewis jumped an amazing 8.91 meters, but then Powell jumped (5)*slight / slightly* further—8.95 meters—to break the world record and win the gold medal. Powell's world record has been unbeaten for over 20 years.

In the past, records were broken all the time. In the 1960s, the long jump record was broken nine times. This was because of improving sports science. The (6)*best/better* shape the athletes were in, the better they performed. However, some scientists believe we're now reaching the end of sports records. What they say (7)*it's / is* that there's a limit to how fast or far a human being can run or jump, and they think that today's athletes are already at that limit.

This phenomenon is (8)*just / quite* as common in women's sports as in men's. In the women's 1500 meters the (9)*faster / fastest* time ever recorded is 3:50.46, a record set by China's Qu Yunxia in 1993. The reason (10)*why / who* Qu's record remains the fastest and Powell's record remains the longest is because that they may be the absolute human maximum for those events.

FUNCTIONAL LANGUAGE
Arguing and making concessions

1 Choose the correct options to complete the underlined phrases.

1 A Matteo's really good at speaking in public, isn't he?
B What? You must be *laughing / joking*! I find his speeches really boring!

2 A I've told you a thousand times that we can't go to the game next week.
B Don't *exaggerate / overestimate*. I forgot that you told me, OK?

3 A I'd like to spend the rest of the budget on building a skating rink.
B I'm not sure *I agree / I'm agreeing* with you there. How many people will use it?

4 A You want to get a new set of golf clubs? That'll cost a fortune!
B I get your *opinion / point*, but it'll be worth it. It will really improve my game.

5 A Getting into the movie industry is impossible if your family isn't in the business.
B Oh, come *on / off*! Lots of people manage to get into it without knowing anyone.

6 A A lot of actors refuse to go on stage unless they have their lucky charm with them.
B That may be the *case / way*, but I'm sure it doesn't make any difference to their performance.

7 A The best athletes are the most dedicated, that's all. They just train harder than their opponents.
B I *propose / suppose* you're right, but don't you think some athletes are just naturally better than the rest?

8 A Isn't Carla a little too old to have that lucky teddy bear? She's nearly nine.
B I understand *what / that* you're saying, but she'd be so upset if I took it away.

2 Complete the chart using the underlined phrases from **1**.

Disagreeing	Making concessions

LISTENING Identifying emotion

1 **a** 9.2 Listen to four conversations. Put a check mark (✓) if one of the speakers is angry or a cross (✗) if neither speaker is angry.

Conversation 1 ☐ Conversation 2 ☐
Conversation 3 ☐ Conversation 4 ☐

b Listen again and choose the correct answer a, b or c.

Conversation 1

1 What does the man not have?
a goggles b a cap c a towel

2 What happens at the end of the conversation?
a The man buys the thing that he needs.
b The man goes home to get the thing that he needs.
c The man leaves the swimming pool and doesn't come back.

Conversation 2

3 Which of these things does the person offer Mariam?
a cheap telephone calls b satellite television
c a WiFi connection

4 How many calls like this has Mariam had today?
a one b three c five

Conversation 3

5 Why didn't Sam win any money?
a He lost his lottery ticket.
b He changed his lottery numbers.
c He forgot to buy a lottery ticket.

6 What did Sam buy yesterday?
a a lottery ticket b a card c a lucky charm

Conversation 4

7 Where was Joe's skateboard stolen?
a on the street b at school
c at the sports center

8 How did Joe get the skateboard?
a It was a present. b He won it.
c He bought it with money from his job.

STRATEGY When you listen, think carefully about how the speakers sound. Are they happy, angry or upset? Identifying a speaker's emotion can help you understand what they're saying.

READING Scanning

1 **a** Each question 1–5 has a word in bold. Find this word in the text to answer the question. Do not read the whole text.

1 How many things does an **American** bride need on her wedding day?

____

2 What do a Tajik bride and groom eat during the wedding **ceremony**?

____

3 What **ritual** does the bride do after the wedding?

____

4 What is ***plov***?

____

5 Why is a **government** official at the wedding?

____

b Read the whole text again. Have these parts of the Tajik wedding ceremony changed recently? Write a check mark (✓) for yes or a cross (✗) for no.

1 The ritual that happens when the guests arrive. ☐
2 The clothing that the bride wears. ☐
3 The preparation of dough by the bride. ☐
4 The number of guests at the wedding. ☐
5 The number of courses at the wedding. ☐
6 The recipe for *plov*. ☐
7 The length of the wedding. ☐
8 The cost of the wedding. ☐

"Something Old, Something New"

"Something old, something new, something borrowed, something blue" is one of the most famous phrases in the English language, representing the four things that every American bride needs for luck on her wedding day. It's a tradition that goes back centuries as weddings remain an unchanging part of society. Weddings in other parts of the world, like Tajikistan, are just as traditional, although change is in the air.

The first thing that happens in a Tajik wedding is the arrival of the guests, who have their hands washed by a member of the family in the traditional way. The bride will appear later, with her face hidden beneath a veil. Then she will join the groom for the ceremony. Once they have made their promises, the couple drinks water and eats a little meat with a pancake to confirm the marriage.

Afterward, the bride says farewell to her family and is escorted to her new home, where she performs an ancient ritual. She takes oil and flour and mixes them to make dough, to show that she is able to cook. She even performs this simple act in her wedding dress. Meanwhile, outside, the guests enjoy a huge festival of music and dance.

From the outside, this event seems almost timeless, but in fact marriages in Tajikistan are changing. There are hard times across the country, and the less work there is available, the harder it is to pay for weddings of this size. In the past, the family might have had to spend an enormous amount of money to pay for the big day. To solve the problem, the government has taken a stand.

In 2011, they introduced a series of new rules. A wedding can have a maximum of 150 guests, and the feast eaten by the guests must only be three hours long. The family is also only allowed to serve a single course. Most people cook *plov*, the traditional dish of Tajikistan, as the sole dish of the day. This delicious dish is a mixture of lamb, rice and vegetables.

These restrictions have been a huge departure from the traditional weddings, which were once among the longest in the world, with festivities continuing for over a week. To enforce the law, there is one extra person attending, a government representative who ensures that the rules are being followed. So far, it seems to have been a success, and it's surely good news for the parents of Tajikistan, who no longer fear being bankrupted by celebrations.

STRATEGY You don't always need to read an entire text to get the information that you need. If you are looking for particular information, scan over the text quickly for key words.

PROGRESS TEST 3

GRAMMAR & VOCABULARY
(25 points)

1 Complete each sentence with one word in each blank (*isn't*, etc. = one word). *(5 points)*

0 The harder you train, *the* easier it will be to run the marathon.
1 My legs are really hurting. I ______ have spent so long in the gym yesterday.
2 You ______ have left your sneakers in the gym, Elnaz. You were wearing them when we left there!
3 Alex's running is improving all the time; he's getting faster and ______ .
4 The ______ I like about running is that you don't need any expensive equipment.
5 ______ I want to know is why the race was canceled.

2 Complete the sentences with the correct form of the word in parentheses. *(5 points)*

0 Gary's not here. He *must have gone* (go) home early today.
1 If I had seen you yesterday, I ________ (invite) you to the office party.
2 If I'd passed all my exams, I ________ (be) in college now.
3 I wish I ________ (have) a job. I hate being here in the unemployment line.
4 I sent my boss a really angry e-mail and then he fired me. If only I ________ (do) that!
5 If I ________ (have) a car, I wouldn't be able to drive to work.

3 a Choose the correct options to complete the sentences. *(5 points)*

0 Our manager was charged with *money* / *tax* evasion. No one was surprised as we all thought he was a *dishonest* (honest) man.
1 You can trust David to *take* / *have* care of any problems with the project. He's very ______ (rely).
2 In some countries, *capital* / *death* punishment is used as a penalty for murder. In other places, this punishment has been made ______ (legal).
3 The tour guide seemed really ______ (trust). We were completely *taken* / *pulled* in by her act. We couldn't believe it when we found out that she'd stolen our wallets!
4 I was really ______ (care) when I filled out my tax *back* / *return*. Now I have to do it again because I made so many mistakes!
5 Three teenagers were arrested *for* / *of* vandalism on the railway line. The police said their behavior was extremely ______ (responsible) because they could have caused an accident.

b Fill in the blanks with the correct form of the words in parentheses. Add a prefix or suffix. *(5 points)*

4 Complete the sentences with the correct form of words from the box. There is one word that you don't need. *(5 points)*

crew club horde jury stroke ~~success~~ swarm

0 Her business has been a great *success* .
1 Don't go outside! There's a ______ of bees in the yard!
2 My mom has to go to court next month because she's going to be on the ______ for a trial.
3 We won $600 in the lottery last year; it was a real ______ of luck.
4 My sister's going to work on the ______ of a cruise ship for six months.
5 We bought Julia some new golf ______ for her birthday.

READING *(25 points)*

1 Read the text on page 61 quickly. What kind of text is it? *(3 points)*

a factual report ☐ b magazine article ☐
c travel guide ☐

2 a Which five countries are mentioned in the text? *(5 points)*

a __________ ______ b __________ ______
c __________ ______ d __________ ______
e __________ ______

b Match the numbers in the box to the countries in **2a**. One country matches two numbers. *(5 points)*

8 13 17 39 49

3 Answer the questions. *(12 points)*

1 What part of his vehicle did the man change in Afghanistan?
____
2 How do the Afghan police feel about this kind of crime?
____
3 What is missing from many apartment buildings in America?
____
4 Why does the author not explain why 13 and 17 are unlucky?
____
5 Which number is considered lucky because of how it is written?
____
6 Why did the Beijing Olympics start on August 8?
____

Lucky for some...

1 I had been working in Afghanistan for a couple of months when, one day, I found my next-door neighbor painting his car license plate. He was calmly removing 39 from the end of it by changing the numbers from black to white. When I asked him whether it was illegal, he just told me it was alright "because the police understand." It seems that the number 39 is very unlucky in his country, and people feel ashamed to be associated with it.

2 In those circumstances, maybe it's not unreasonable to change your car license plate. This kind of thing happens all over the world. In the States many apartment blocks don't have a thirteenth floor because it's considered unlucky! It may seem foolish and superstitious, but it does make business sense. If people won't buy an apartment on the thirteenth floor, there's no reason to have one!

3 Strangely enough, in Italy, it's the number 17 that you need to be careful about! So there isn't a row of seats with that number on Alitalia planes, for example. Just like lucky rituals, it's hard to say where these superstitions come from. There are so many theories, it would be impossible for me to explain them all here!

4 In Asia, these superstitions are often related to language. In Japan, you're very unlikely to find a hotel room with the number 49 because those numbers together sound like the word for death. People don't want to think about such negative subjects while they're on vacation.

5 On the other hand, they love the number eight because its Japanese character shows two expanding lines. The idea is that they mean "prosperity." Across the sea in China, people also think of this number as the key to wealth and success. It's so popular that organizers decided to open the Beijing Olympics at 8 a.m. on August 8, 2008. Perhaps the number really is lucky because they were one of the best Olympics in history!

LISTENING *(25 points)*

1 T3 Listen to a radio news report. Which crimes does the presenter talk about? Number the crimes 1–5. There is one crime that you don't need. *(5 points)*

arson	☐	murder	☐
burglary	☐	trespassing	☐
illegal file sharing	☐	vandalism	☐

2 Listen again. Answer the questions. *(20 points)*

0 What were the protestors trying to enter?
A nuclear power station.

1 How old were the protestors?
____

2 When were the protesters allowed to go home?
____

3 What was damaged in New Town?
____

4 What punishment can people now get for this kind of crime?
____

5 How many warnings do people get before their Internet service is stopped?
____

6 How many computers have already been disconnected?
____

7 How much will the repairs at Good Hope High School cost?
____

8 Who was responsible for starting the fire?
____

9 What job did Bruce Twining use to do?
____

10 What punishment did Roger Churchill receive?
____

WRITING *(25 points)*

1 Complete the words in the blog post. *(5 points)*

Home | Blog | Links | Photos | About | Contact

When soccer fans get together at the stadium, they turn into a mob. Their behavior can become irresponsible, disrespectful and even violent; they often cause damage and disruption in the local area. In (1)a _ _ _ _ _ _ _ n , they give the sport a bad reputation. Of (2)c _ _ _ _ _ , I'm not saying that the people who go to soccer games behave like this every day. There's no (3)q _ _ _ _ _ _ _ that their actions change because they're part of a large group of people: psychologists have (4)f _ _ _ d that people behave differently when they're in a crowd. I couldn't (5)a _ _ _ _ more with people who say that punishments for this behavior should be tougher. In my opinion, "herd mentality" isn't an excuse.

posted by CarlosV at 13:59

2 Write a blog post. Reply to the post in **1**, giving your opinion. *(20 points)*

10 VALUE FOR MONEY

VOCABULARY

Phrasal verbs about money

1 Complete the online chat with the correct form of the phrasal verbs from the box.

cut back	fork out	get by	pay off
rip off	run out of	save up	take out

Today's online chat is with retail expert Ann Dobson. Join us live from 4 p.m. GMT.

I Many families find it difficult to (1) ______ financially. How can people (2) ______ on their spending to reduce their supermarket bill?

A Well, many people go shopping when they (3) ______ something essential like flour. This is a bad idea if you haven't eaten. Never go to the supermarket hungry, or you'll (4) ______ on lots of things you don't really need.

I So do supermarkets (5) ______ their customers—make them pay more than the fair price?

A Not really, but they have little tricks to encourage people to buy more.

I I see.

A Sometimes supermarkets help, though. With a store card, you get points every time you shop. If you (6) ______ your points, you can get bargains in the future.

I And what about a shopping list?

A A list is essential. Plan your shopping before going to the supermarket, then only buy things on your list. Otherwise there are so many things to buy. You don't want to (7) ______ a loan just to pay for your weekly food shopping! Another tip: leave cards at home. I knew one man who had trouble (8) ______ his credit card bills every month. He started only taking cash to the supermarket to stop overspending.

I Ann, thanks for your advice!

Materials

2 Find 14 materials in the word search.

V	P	O	L	Y	E	S	T	E	R
A	L	E	A	T	H	E	R	C	U
L	A	S	T	E	E	L	Z	A	B
U	S	Q	S	W	O	O	L	R	B
M	T	D	I	K	Z	B	J	D	E
I	I	J	L	Q	J	K	W	B	R
N	C	L	K	F	G	D	A	O	N
U	V	B	V	K	Z	V	X	A	R
M	J	N	Y	L	O	N	Q	R	P
M	A	H	O	G	A	N	Y	D	I
F	U	H	S	C	O	T	T	O	N
A	M	K	T	Y	S	L	D	I	E

3 Choose the correct options to complete the sentences.

1 *Aluminum / Mahogany* is a very useful metal.
2 Scientists invented *nylon / silk* in the twentieth century.
3 I always wear *rubber / wool* gloves when I wash the dishes.
4 I prefer clothes that are made from natural fibers like *polyester / cotton*.
5 Many candles are made out of *cardboard / wax*.
6 Sarah always buys *leather / plastic* shoes because she doesn't want to wear animal products.
7 *Steel / Pine* is often used in large building projects because it's very strong.

Adjective order

4 Put the adjectives in parentheses in the right order to complete the ads. Do you ever write ads like these?

(1) ______________ (*black / stylish / leather*) jacket for sale. Size 38. Contact me at ep23@email.com.

FOR SALE – (2) ______________ (*round / dining / large / pine*) table. Excellent condition!

Now available—a set of (3) ______________ (*rare / American / old*) postcards, some very valuable. Call 5780-1922 for more info.

(4) ______________ (*Italian / mountain / secondhand*) bike for sale, only $69. A real bargain!

Business & finance

5 Match 1–5 to a–e to making questions.

1 How did you get the capital ____
2 When did you start running ____
3 Did you get a grant ____
4 What service ____
5 What are your company's ____

a do you provide?
b to start the business?
c day-to-day expenses?
d from the government?
e your business?

6 **a** Read the interview with a businesswoman. Complete a–e with the questions from **5**.

Today I'm talking to Mette Lund, successful businesswoman and company owner.

(a) ____________________

I started the business when I was nineteen because I needed to pay my (1) ____________ through college. I didn't want to get into (2) ____________ if I could avoid it!

(b) ____________________

We help people and companies who want to recycle old technology equipment. The metals used in things like cell phones can be worth a lot of money.

(c) ____________________

At first, I used my savings; I started with about $400! Later, I persuaded local companies to (3) ____________ in the business.

(d) ____________________

No, we didn't. We did borrow money from the bank, though. I'm starting to repay that (4) ____________ now that the company is making a (5) ____________ . In the first few years, we didn't make any money. We just had enough to (6) ____________ our operating expenses.

(e) ____________________

Renting our office space and staff salaries. We try to give our employees good (7) ____________, and we regularly send them to training courses.

Well thanks very much, Mette. We hope the business continues to grow!

b Complete 1–7 with words from the box. There is one word that you don't need.

benefits cover debt invest loan profit return way

Vocabulary Extension
Further materials

7 **a** Match the objects in the box to materials 1–6. Some objects match more than one material.

cup floor statue tile wire

1 concrete ____________

2 copper ____________

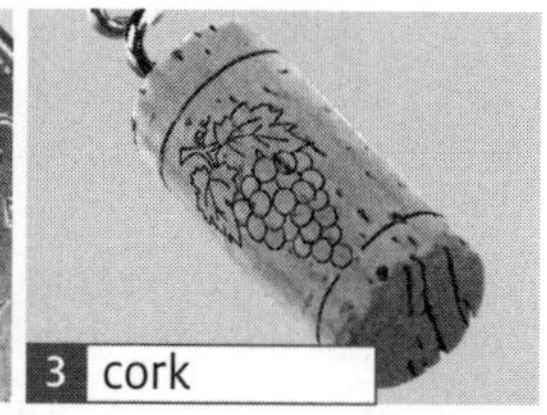
3 cork ____________

4 marble ____________

5 ceramic ____________

6 polystyrene ____________

b Can you think of any other objects that are made with these materials?

8 **a** Complete the sentences with a material from **7a**.

1 A lot of food and drink packaging is made of ______ .
2 The old temple downtown is made of beautiful white ______ .
3 ______ is often used to make electrical wire.
4 Bottles of wine or oil often have tops made of ______ .
5 There are too many ugly gray ______ buildings in this city.
6 The walls of the villa are decorated with painted ______ tiles.

b 10.1 Listen and check.

Bring It Together

9 Choose the correct options to complete the text.

→→Save! Save! Save!←←

With our top money-saving tips, you'll never be ripped (1)*off / up*!

Tip #1 Sign up for websites like Groupon, which offers discounts in local stores and restaurants. They (2)*provide / perform* a great service for people who want to save money.

Tip #2 Think carefully before you fork (3)*up / out* big bills on (4)*big expensive / expensive big* purchases like furniture or a piece of technology. If you want a new (5)*pine / polystyrene* dining table, or the (6)*digital latest / latest digital* camera, find out when the stores will be having their next sale. Stores often lower their prices after big holidays.

Tip #3 If you're trying to save (7)*back / up* some money, be prepared to change your bank account fairly regularly. This can help you get the highest (8) *repay / return* on the money you invest.

If you have a great money-saving tip, share it here! Write a comment

GRAMMAR

Either… or/neither… nor

1 Choose the correct options to complete the text.

Must go Moscow

Moscow is a real treat for architecture fans. If you go on a trip to the Russian capital, you can (1)*either / or* spend your time looking at modern buildings, (2)*and / or* medieval buildings from the country's past. Red Square in the center is a perfect place to start your trip. You can (3)*either / neither* go shopping in the GUM superstore on one side of the square, (4)*or / nor* visit The Kremlin and its museums on the other side. Tourists always go to this area, but for me (5)*either / neither* building is as impressive as the Seven Sisters. These are a group of buildings that were built from 1947 to 1953. One of the most famous is the Russian Foreign Ministry building. Unfortunately, you can (6)*either / neither* go inside it (7)*nor / or* take a guided tour. You just have to take photographs outside. However, one of the group is the Hotel Leningradskaya. You can (8)*either / neither* spend the night here (9)*or / nor* just have a meal in its beautiful restaurant. Be careful though—(10)*either / neither* one is cheap, and this is not an option for the budget traveler!

2 Match comments 1–6 to a–f.

1 The hotel was terrible! It was neither near the beach ____
2 What are you doing for the party? You can either bring some snacks ____
3 Someone is going to be the new manager. It's either going to me ____
4 You can either pay in cash ____
5 I was very upset with the course. The teachers were neither friendly ____
6 The city wasn't very interesting. It had neither a museum ____

a nor in the downtown area.
b or Griselda Vílchez.
c nor an art gallery.
d or by credit card.
e nor well-prepared.
f or some paper plates and polystyrene cups.

3 Complete the comments from a customer survey using the words in parentheses. Remember to use the correct form of the verbs.

Do you ever use our online shopping service? How can we improve it? We'd love to hear your ideas!

I usually find that (1) ________ the website (2) ________ my computer (3) ________ while I'm trying to pay! So I prefer to buy things in the store. (crash / either / or)

I think the online service works really well. It's great that I can (4) ________ online (5) ________ the store downtown. (shop / or / visit / either)

No, I never shop online. In my opinion, it's (6) ________ quicker, (7) ________ easier! There always seem to be problems. (nor / neither)

I think you need to keep more products in stock. Sometimes (8) ________ the online store (9) ________ your branches in town (10) ________ the things I'm looking for! (have / neither / nor)

Articles

4 Complete the sentences with *a*, *an*, *the* or Ø (= no article).

1 There was ____ letter for you this morning. ____ envelope said it was from Chile.
2 Who was ____ man you met in ____ Hotel Suiza?
3 Health experts warn people that ____ fruit juice contains a lot of ____ sugar.
4 You look exhausted. You need to take ____ vacation or ____ day off or something.
5 You can stay in ____ bedroom on the top floor of the house. It's my daughter's, but she's studying at ____ university at the moment.
6 I saw ____ amazing silk shirt this morning. It was ____ coolest shirt that I've ever seen.
7 I want to get ____ cat, but my parents don't like ____ pets.
8 ____ Indus river begins in ____ Himalayas.

5 Which sentences are correct? Mark (✓) the correct box: a, b or both a and b.

1 a Dad's gone to the store to buy newspaper.
  b Dad's in the living room reading the newspaper.
  a ☐ b ☐ both a and b ☐
2 a There's something wrong with my ankle. It hurts.
  b The doctor needs to look at the ankle that's hurting you.
  a ☐ b ☐ both a and b ☐
3 a I need to buy a cell phone. Mine's not working.
  b Some people believe that the cell phones are bad for your health.
  a ☐ b ☐ both a and b ☐
4 a Nile is the longest river in the world.
  b The Pacific is the largest ocean on Earth.
  a ☐ b ☐ both a and b ☐
5 a I saw a fabulous vase in the market, so I haggled with the vendor to get a better price.
  b The best place to get a bargain is January sales.
  a ☐ b ☐ both a and b ☐
6 a My sister works in the hospital because she's a surgeon.
  b I have to go into hospital for an operation on the knee.
  a ☐ b ☐ both a and b ☐

6 Choose the correct options to complete the e-mail. (Ø = no article).

Hi Elka

How's (1)*the / Ø* life in Germany? I haven't seen you since we left (2)*a / Ø* college! That's six months now! Anyway, since then I've been working as (3)*a / the* waitress in a restaurant. It's (4)*a / Ø* good job, but I'm a little bored, and I want to do something more challenging. Anyway, yesterday I saw (5)*an / the* advertisement in the newspaper saying that there were jobs in Germany. (6)*An / The* ad said that anyone who spoke English could apply. It's with a company that is in (7)*the / Ø* Black Forest. That's really near your hometown, isn't it? If they ask me to come for (8)*an / Ø* interview, can I stay at your house? If you don't have (9)*a / the* spare room, I can always sleep on (10)*the / Ø* sofa. That's no problem for me. Would that be OK?

Hope to hear from you soon!

Isobel

Bring It Together

7 Complete the text with one word in each blank (*isn't*, etc. = one word).

My World

Nguyen Van Son

Floating Markets

Floating markets are a common sight in my country, Vietnam, especially along (1)______ Mekong River. (2)______ busiest of all of them is the market at Phung Hiep, where you can see hundreds of boats fighting for trade. You can (3)______ eat hot food cooked on the boat, or you can buy fresh ingredients to cook at home. My grandmother worked at the market for years as (4)______ cook, and I still think of her hot soup whenever I go there.

An important thing about the market is its schedule. Neither the fruit traders (5)______ the fisherman work after 11 a.m., so you have to get there early. Many tourists here take (6)______ tour around the market, and I recommend that, too. If you don't speak Vietnamese, you'll (7)______ be able to speak to people nor get the best prices for things. Bargaining is (8)______ big part of market life, so grab a local guide and let them get all the deals for you!

FUNCTIONAL LANGUAGE
Arranging for a service

1 Complete the words in the conversations.

1
A We'd like to rent some mountain bikes tomorrow. Can you tell me your daily [1]r __ t __ ?
B The normal bikes are $15 a day, and the mountain bikes are $30.
A OK, and what's your minimum rental [2]p __ r __ __ d?
B There isn't one. You can rent them for as long as you like.
A Great! Will I need to pay a [3]d __ p __ __ __ t, too?
B Yes, it's $70 per person per bike.
A No problem. And one more question. What [4]d __ c __ m __ __ __ s do I need?
B We'll need to see your passport or an identity card. OK?
A Yes, that's fine. Thanks very much for your help.

2
C I'd like to get an [1]e __ __ __ m __ __ e for replacing the carpet in my bedroom. It's really old.
D Certainly. Do you have a [2]b __ d __ __ t for the job?
C Yes, I do. I can't really pay more than about $200.
D Well I think we can do that.
C Is there a [3]d __ __ c __ __ nt if I pay cash?
D No, I'm afraid there isn't. Now, you need to choose the carpet first. I'll show you some samples.
C Oh I don't have a car. Can I arrange for the carpet to be [4]d __ l __ v __ __ __ d?
D Yes, yes, don't worry about that. We'll handle everything.
C Great. OK, let's look at the samples then.

LISTENING
Listening for stress

1 **a** Look at this introduction to an interview on shopping rip-offs. Underline the words that you think will be stressed the most.

b 10.2 Listen and check.

2 10.3 Listen to the rest of the interview and correct the wrong information.

1 The prices of parking change a lot during the day, and there are special deals, too.
2 It's best to go online to find the cheapest train tickets.
3 If you want to get something on sale, you have to go early in the morning.
4 Here's a tip: sales often begin on a Monday when most people are at work.
5 You've been shopping all day for a new leather jacket. You've found neither the right color nor the right design.
6 How much do you pay for a hot chocolate? $3?
7 Well that's true, but with a 100% profit the café soon pays for all that!

STRATEGY In English, the most important words in a sentence always receive more stress than other words in the sentence. When you listen, try to pick out these key words and use them to help you understand the whole conversation.

WRITING A CV

Bernice Omanuwa
15 Pickle Street
Durham
DH18 1PW

Home tel.	(0191) 4980904
Cel.	(07700) 900211
E-mail	bernice@berniceomanuwa.com
1 ________	Nigerian
2 ________	March 1, 1986

3 ________

2012–	**Import Manager, Kamble Imports** Manager for imports of wooden furniture to the UK and Europe. Responsible for liaising with suppliers in China, Nigeria and South Africa. Several successes in achieving new contracts in Wales and Ireland.
2010–2011	**Sales Manager, Worley Candles** Sales Manager for Worley Candles, which involved dealing with stores throughout the UK. Also developed new range of colorful candles for storefront displays. Managed a team of seven people.
2009–2010	**Salesperson, Worley Candles** Handled orders for the Perceive Candle Range from Nigeria to suppliers in northwest England and Scotland.

4 ________

2004–2008	**BA Hons in Marketing** Durham Business School, Durham University
2001–2004	**Castlemount School, London** A level math (A), English (A), economics (A), Chinese (C) 11 GCSEs (Grade A).

5 ________

Dance	Member of local salsa club in Durham. I take part in regular performances with my dance group.
Travel	My dream is to travel to every country in the world.

6 ________

Valid driver's license.
Fluent in English and Hausa.
Intermediate level Chinese.
Basic programming (Java, C++).

1 Fill in blanks 1–6 in the CV with headings from the box.

Date of birth Education
Hobbies and interests Nationality
Other skills Work experience

2 Read the CV again and answer the questions.

1. What did Bernice study at the university?
2. How many languages does she speak?
3. What computer skills does she have?
4. What does she do in her spare time?
5. How long has she worked at her current company?
6. How many people was she in charge of in her previous job?
7. What was her weakest school subject when she was 18?
8. What's her zip code?

3 **a** What information would you include in your CV? Prepare notes about...

- personal information
- work experience
- education
- hobbies and interests
- other skills

b Write your CV. Be careful to organize your work clearly.

STRATEGY When you write a CV, it's important to organize your ideas carefully. Your CV needs to be clear and easy to read so that it makes a good impression. Make sure you include key information about your skills and experience, but don't write too much. Try to limit it to one page.

11 TECHNOLOGY

VOCABULARY
Talking about ideas & inventions

1 Read the text and complete the words.

Currently working on...
a flying carpet!

Flying carpets may become a reality, according to Professor Lakshminarayanan Mahadevan of Harvard University. His flash of inspiration came from observing the movements of rays, a type of fish that swims close to the ocean floor. Mahadevan's (1) b _ _ _ kt _ _ _ _ _ gh was to apply this observation to movement in the air. He believes it would be possible to make a "flying" sheet large enough to carry a person, but it would have one major (2) d _ _ wb _ _ k: it wouldn't be very comfortable to ride on! Of course there might be some (3) e _ _ ly a _ _ p _ ers who would be willing to try it, but many feel that the flying carpet idea is just a (4) _ imm _ _ k. However, this technology could still become a (5) co _ _ er c _ al su _ _ ess. Some people have suggested that flexible, flying sheets could be used in machines and other useful (6) g _ d _ _ ts.

2 Complete the sentences with the adjective formed from the noun in parentheses. Add *-al* and/or *un-* if necessary.

1 I remember watching a program about astronomy that was really ______________. It made me want to learn all I could about the universe. (inspiration)

2 The ______________ idea came from a researcher in France and was then developed by a team in the U.S. (origin)

3 New technology has meant that many ______________ ways of working have disappeared. (tradition)

4 I think it's ______________ to communicate just by writing on social networks. Human beings are meant to speak to each other. (nature)

5 There is a new type of soft, flexible robot that is very different from the ______________, metallic one. (convention)

6 The keys on most keyboards are in an ______________ order. It doesn't make any sense! (logic)

3 Complete the conversation with the correct form of the verbs from the box.

come	figure	get	strike

A Do you like my T-shirt? I printed it myself.

B Really? It's so unusual! How did you (1) ______ up with the design?

A I saw some similar designs on a website, and it (2) ______ me that I could create my own.

B Was it difficult?

A No, not really, although it took a while to (3) ______ out which colors to use!

B How did you print the design onto the fabric?

A I (4) ______ the idea for that from a craft website. I used a special kind of paper and an iron!

B You should start a business making them!

Describing gadgets

4 a Unscramble the letters in parentheses to make words.

The TouchTunes Virtuo is a jukebox for the twenty-first century. OK, it doesn't have the same shiny (1) ____________ (latmelic) case of the 1950s' original or the (2) ____________ (nudored) glass cover that keeps the records inside. In fact, this music player is more similar to portable, (3) ____________ (lehdnadh) gadgets like MP3 players or smartphones. This (4) ____________ (gihh-htce) product allows users to access huge digital music libraries and to search for songs by genre or lyrics. There are no buttons to press. The screen is (5) ____________ (cuhto-tinsvseei) and designed to be operated by someone's finger. It's also incredibly (6) ____________ (lmsi), so it hangs on the wall like a picture. The music isn't "small" though—the sound quality is incredible!

b Look at the photos. Can you think of any other adjectives to describe the gadgets?

Vocabulary Extension

Computing words

5 **a** Read the definitions. Complete the sentences with the words and phrases in bold.

backup a copy of your files that you make in case your computer doesn't work

boot up to restart a computer

bug a mistake in a computer program that stops it from working correctly

crash to stop working suddenly (of a computer)

hard copy a paper copy of a file that is on your computer or online

jargon technical language used by experts that is not easily understood by other people

shut down to turn off your computer when you finish using it

user-friendly easy to use by people, straightforward

1 It's very important for gadgets to be ____________ as people want to be able to use them quickly and easily.
2 I wish someone would explain what all this ____________ means so that I can choose the computer that I need.
3 You should always make a ____________ of your files in case your laptop gets stolen.
4 I'll find the website for you in a moment. I just need to ____________ the computer.
5 My computer doesn't ____________ often. It's usually very reliable.
6 We have some new software at work that is causing us a lot of problems. Every week we find a new ____________ in it.
7 I forgot to ____________ my computer before I went to bed, so it was on all night.
8 Could you send me a ____________ of that document, please? My printer's not working at the moment.

b 11.1 Listen and check.

6 Complete the e-mail with the correct forms of the words and phrases in **5a**.

Hi Alberto,
Help! Something's wrong with my computer. Yesterday, I was surfing the Internet when my laptop suddenly (1) ________________ . The picture stopped moving, and it wouldn't even (2) ________________ : I had to take the battery out to stop it! Now, whenever I start the computer, it won't (3) ________________ . In the beginning, I thought it was a virus, but a colleague of mine told me it was probably a (4) ________________ in the program. She printed off some instructions from the Internet for me and gave me the (5) ________________ . But the instructions aren't (6) ________________ at all! They're all written in specialist (7) ________________ , and I don't understand them. Could you come over tomorrow and look at my laptop for me? All my files are on it, and if I can't use it, I'll lose months of work because, stupidly, I never made a (8) ________________ .
Please help!
Morgan

Done

Bring It Together

7 Choose the correct options to complete the article.

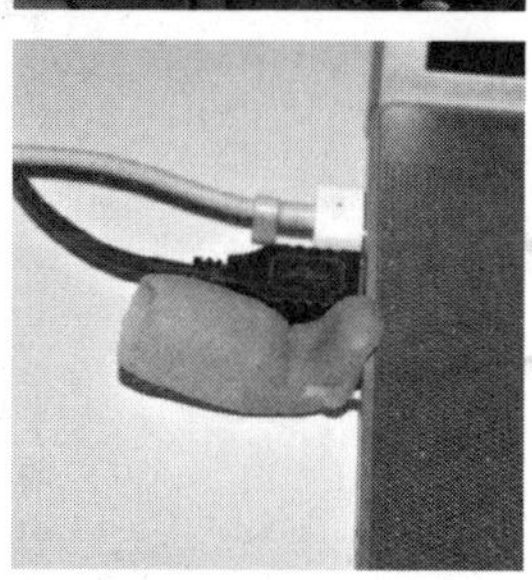

The easiest way to make a (1) *backup* / *hard copy* of the files on your computer is to save them on a separate device, like a flash drive. However, there is one big (2) *instruction* / *drawback* to using these small, portable drives—they're very easy to lose. This isn't a problem for Finnish computer programmer Jerry Jalava, though—his flash drive is one of his fingers! When Jerry lost his finger in a motorcycle accident, his doctors joked that he should have a "finger drive." Jalava then (3) *struck* / *figured* out a way of making an artificial finger with a USB drive attached. It's not a (4) *gimmick* / *bug*. He uses the flash drive to store photos, movies and other files. He even has plans to make another, more (5) *high-tech* / *high-technology* drive with WiFi and more storage. This "handheld" device is certainly (6) *unconventional* / *traditional*!

GRAMMAR
Relative clauses

1 **a** Choose the correct option to complete the sentences. Sometimes both options are correct.

1 Let me show you the present *that* / *who* I've bought for Javier.
2 I need to find someone *who* / *which* speaks Chinese.
3 That's the architect *whose* / *which* design won an innovation award.
4 Is he the programmer *that* / *who* started the software company?
5 The place *that* / *who* serves the best coffee is the little café on the corner.
6 This website has lots of unusual gadgets *who* / *that* might appeal to you.
7 I think the phone number *that* / *who* I gave you is wrong.
8 A gadget *that* / *who* has really changed my life is my smartphone.

b In which sentences, 1–8, can we omit the relative pronoun? ______________

3 Add commas to sentences 1–8 if necessary.

1 I need to find a store where I can buy spare parts for my camera.
2 There is only one drawback to this tablet which is that the battery doesn't last very long.
3 My dad who works for a big IT company always helps me solve my computer problems.
4 We need a faster broadband speed that will let us watch streamed video more easily.
5 Apple which was started by Steve Jobs and Steve Wozniak is now the most profitable computer company in the world.
6 I need to speak to someone who can explain this IT jargon to me.
7 Bill Gates whose Microsoft products are sold all over the world gives huge sums of money to global health and education programs.
8 Large numbers of people now have cell phones which has led publishers to create cell phone games that are fun to play.

2 Complete the text with one word in each blank.

aimi eguchi – number 1 cyber star

In early 2011, Japanese music fans were all talking about Aimi Eguchi, (1)__________ had just joined the pop group AKB48. She was the girl (2)__________ voice was more beautiful than the other girls'. Almost immediately, she began to play a big role in the band's TV show, (3)__________ amazed fans across the country.

After a while, bloggers started to realize why Aimi was so perfect: she didn't really exist!

Aimi was actually a computer-generated character (4)__________ had been created from all the other band members. Bloggers began posting photos of Aimi's face to show the features (5)__________ had been copied from other girls in the band. Her songs, (6)__________ had been recorded by an actor, were digitally adjusted. All the information about her life (7)__________ was on the band's website had been invented, too. She wasn't born in 1995 in Saitama but rather on the keyboards of a team of clever designers. Fans of hers were shocked by the revelation, (8)__________ is hardly surprising. It now remains to be seen whether Aimi will be the beginning of a trend of pixelated pop stars.

So/such

4 Complete the conversation with *so* or *such*.

TREVOR	Good morning, this is Trevor Jones.
MOM	Hello, Trevor.
TREVOR	Oh, hi Mom. How are you?
MOM	I'm all right. How are you? It's been (1) __________ a long time since I last heard from you.
TREVOR	I'm fine, thanks. Mom, you know I'm at work, don't you?
MOM	Yes, yes. I just wanted to check that you got my e-mail yesterday.
TREVOR	I did, yes. I haven't had time to reply yet. Sorry. I've been really busy. I have (2) __________ much work to do.
MOM	Do you? Your sister does, too. You're both working (3) __________ hard at the moment. Nicole couldn't come home last weekend because she had to work. It was (4) __________ a shame because we went to see your Auntie Ellen in her new house.
TREVOR	Yes, in your e-mail you said you were sending me some pictures of the house, but there weren't any with the message.
MOM	Oh! I know how that happened! I was in (5) __________ a rush that I forgot to send them. I'll send them to you now. I took (6) __________ many photos! Her house is (7) __________ beautiful. We had (8) __________ a lovely afternoon there, sitting on her patio.
TREVOR	That's great. Look Mom, I'd better go now. I'll call you later, OK?
MOM	Oh, yes, of course, dear. Bye!

5 Put *enough* in the correct place to complete the sentences.

1 The computer isn't powerful for the game that I bought.
2 There isn't space here for a music system.
3 I bought a new PC because my old one didn't have a large memory.
4 Do we have food for all the visitors to the IT conference?
5 Matt is talented to run his own software company.

BRING IT TOGETHER

6 a Complete the blog post with the words from the box. There is one word that you don't need.

enough	so	such (x2)
that (x)	who	whose

Space Debris

Space is (1) __________ empty that you could travel for light-years and see nothing. That's the theory. Unfortunately, it's no longer true. Since 1957, when the Russians sent the first satellite, ***Sputnik***, into space, thousands of other objects have been left in orbit. Many of these are large (2) __________ to do serious damage if they hit other objects. This is a real possibility: in 2011 the International Space Station, (3) __________ crew carries out important research, was almost hit by some debris, and the crew nearly had to return to Earth. Space debris has become (4) __________ a big problem that a number of companies are trying to find ways of removing it. One (5) __________ company is Star Inc. The spacecraft (6) __________ they are developing is called the EDDE (Electro Dynamic Debris Eliminator) Vehicle. This is a spacecraft (7) __________ can capture space debris with lightweight nets. However, a machine (8) __________ can pick up trash in space, can also pick up other things, including other countries' satellites. Star Inc. therefore wants EDDE to be controlled by the United Nations so that all the world's governments will support their plan to make space a greener place for everyone!

debris /debriː/ (noun) large pieces of stone, metal, wood, etc., that have been left in an area after an accident or a disaster (e.g., an earthquake)

b Which relative pronoun in the text can be omitted?

FUNCTIONAL LANGUAGE
Dealing with technical problems

1 Complete the conversation with the correct form of the words from the box.

already	manage	mean	say	suppose	try

A Jackie, you're the computer guru. Can you help me with something?
B Yeah! What's the problem?
A I want to put a music program on my tablet. I downloaded it this morning, but it doesn't work. I've finally (1) ____________ to get it started, but I can't get any sound.
B That's strange. What's the program (2) ____________ to do?
A To replicate the sounds of musical instruments. It (3) ____________ that it's compatible with this tablet.
B What about reinstalling it?
A I've (4) ____________ tried that, but it didn't work.
B Have you (5) ____________ looking on the Internet? Maybe other people have had the same problem. Let's take a look. They say here that you're (6) ____________ to download some software before using the program.
A Really? And then it'll work?
B I think so. Let's give it a try, shall we?

LISTENING
Listening to longer conversations

1 **a** 11.2 Look at the photo and take notes about the questions.

1 Where are the people?
2 What job do you think they do?
3 What kind of questions do you think they have to answer?

b Listen and check your ideas.

2 Listen again and choose the correct answer a, b or c.

1 Where was Nikhil when he was given the leaflet for the job?
   a outside the university library
   b outside a computer store
   c outside the call center
2 What does Nikhil say about his salary at the call center?
   a They were very high.
   b They were very low.
   c They were average.
3 What was not shown on the computer on the wall of the call center?
   a the length of each call
   b the number of people waiting
   c the name and address of the caller
4 Which of these people did Nikhil not like in this job?
   a his boss
   b the customers
   c his coworkers
5 What was wrong with one customer's handheld games player?
   a It was completely broken.
   b There was a cable missing.
   c The battery hadn't been charged.
6 Why couldn't one customer install the program she wanted?
   a There was something wrong with the disk.
   b She didn't have the disk.
   c She'd put the disk into the wrong place.
7 Why didn't one man's computer boot up?
   a He hadn't turned it on.
   b It had a virus.
   c There was a problem with the screen.
8 Where does Nikhil work now?
   a in a design company
   b in another call center
   c in a software company

STRATEGY When you listen to a long conversation, you won't always understand everything, but don't panic!
- Listen for key information to answer the questions.
- Think about the context of the audio. Does this give you any clues about what the speakers are saying?
- Don't stop listening if you hear a word that you don't understand.

READING Using pictures

1 **a** Look at images 1–4 and choose the best sentence to describe the machine.

a The Thing-O-Matic is used to make 3D images of plastic objects so that you can keep the images on your computer.
b The Thing-O-Matic is used to make plastic objects at home, with the help of your computer.
c The Thing-O-Matic is used to clean objects using special chemicals.

b Read the text and check your answers.

2 Fill in the blanks in the text with sentences a–g. There is one sentence that you do not need.

a That takes most people about twelve hours, apparently.
b It can even make spare parts for itself!
c This USB cable transfers the data to the machine, just like a normal printer.
d It was a disaster with no solution in sight.
e White layers began to appear on a kind of moving platform.
f The project is in development right now, but it could be on the market within five years.
g He's the kind of man who takes a whole week to put an Ikea chest of drawers together.

I think I'll just make a thingamajig...

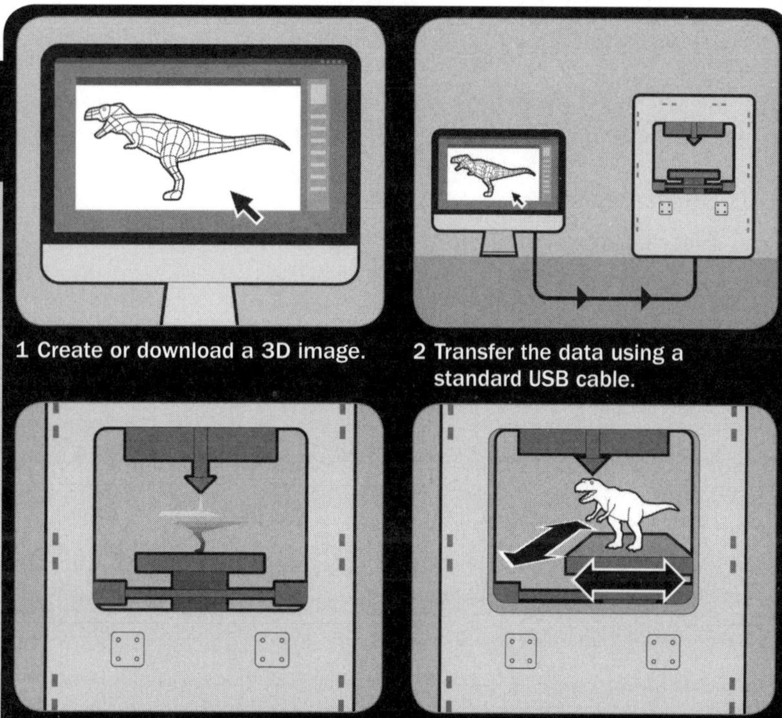

1 Create or download a 3D image.
2 Transfer the data using a standard USB cable.
3 Hot plastic is sprayed in layers through a nozzle.
4 The platform below the object moves.

My four-year-old daughter was sitting on the floor crying. We were at my friend Ali's house, and his dog had just bitten the head off her favorite toy, a plastic dinosaur. (1)______ That was until Ali told us to follow him with the cryptic comment, "Don't worry about your T-Rex. I'll make you a new one!"

Feeling slightly suspicious, we all followed him to the garage where he showed us a wooden box that was connected to his computer. When Ali told me he had built this device from a kit, I could hardly believe my eyes. (2)______ Now he was telling us that he had made this machine: the Thing-O-Matic.

Ali put the dinosaur on a special device and created a 3D image of it on his computer. Once this was done, he sent the image to this mysterious box that began to whirr and vibrate. Then hot plastic shot out of a special nozzle. (3)______ Before our eyes, an exact replica of the dinosaur began to appear. To my daughter, it was nothing short of magic (and to be honest, it felt the same to me, too).

The amazing thing is that the Thing-O-Matic is available for anyone who wants one. It can be ordered though the mail for $1,599, which includes all the software you need. The only drawback is that you have to assemble it yourself. (4)______ But if Ali can do it, anyone can.

The machine was created by MakerBot Industries in New York City. It can produce toys, tools, or almost anything in plastic. (5)______

The really exciting thing about the Thing-O-Matic is that this is just the beginning. At the moment, the main innovation is that it can model things in plastic, but it could soon work with metals and other materials, too. There is even the possibility that a similar device could make an entire cell phone. And there's not long to wait until you can buy one! (6)______ Tell me that isn't magic! My daughter certainly thinks so!

STRATEGY Reading texts often include pictures or photos. Study these images carefully before you read to help you understand any new vocabulary or complicated descriptions.

12 Out of the Ordinary

Vocabulary

Experiences

1 Circle the word that doesn't work in each conversation.

1 A What was the best moment of your trip to Costa Rica?
B I remember one morning when we were camping and I woke up very early. It was *dawn / sunrise / twilight*, and the rain forest was absolutely beautiful.

2 A Do you remember our trip to Iceland?
B Oh yeah—walking along the beach *in the dead of night / at dusk / at twilight*, just as it was getting dark. Magic!

3 A You look exhausted, Miriam! What's wrong?
B I didn't get much sleep last night. I had to get up at *daybreak / at sunset / in the dead of night* to drive my brother to the airport. He had a 6 a.m. flight!

4 A What's your favorite time of day?
B Well, I love *dusk / late afternoon / midmorning*. On weekends I love sitting in the garden in the bright sunshine and just taking it easy.

5 A What do you like to do when you finish work in the evening?
B I like to walk home along the riverbank where I can look at the mountains *at dawn / at sunset / at dusk*.

6 A What time should I call you tomorrow?
B Well, I'm busy all afternoon, so *early morning / late afternoon / midmorning* would be best.

2 Complete the adjectives and intensifiers in the e-mail.

New | Reply Reply all Forward | Delete Junk Sweep Mark as Move to

To Betty

Hello from Arizona! We visited the Grand Canyon yesterday; it was (1)a __ e __ __ __ e! We drove there and the whole trip was (2)a __ s __ l __ t __ __ y (3)b __ __ __ tht __ k __ __ g. We had to drive on mountain roads with no walls to protect us in case of an accident! But it was worth it because the Canyon is really (4)__ w __ -in __ __ ir __ __ g. The views are truly spectacular. The best moment was at dusk—watching the sun go down over the rocks was a (5)t __ t __ __ __ __ (6)o __ __ rw __ __ __ __ __ __ g experience. I have some (7)st __ __ n __ __ g photos to show you when we get back!

Love,

Lucy

3 **a** Match 1–4 to a–d to make four expressions.

1 Riding in a helicopter over São Paolo at dusk. That memory really sticks ___
2 When I saw my beautiful wife on our wedding day. She really took ___
3 Going to my first football game at the stadium. When I saw the crowd, I couldn't believe ___
4 When I was invited to watch a movie being filmed. It was a once ___

a out to me.
b my eyes!
c in a lifetime experience.
d my breath away.

b What question do you think the people in **3a** are answering?

Night expressions

4 Complete the text with the words from the box. There is one word that you don't need.

call	crack	get	long	nights	overnight	shift	sleep	stay

Hidden Dangers

In my job I often have to work the night (1)_________ . This means working all night (2)_________ , five nights a week. It pays well, but I've read that working (3)_________ can be bad for your health. Apparently, you're more likely to suffer from obesity, diabetes and heart disease. The article explained that these risks don't affect people who occasionally (4)_________ up all night at a party or go on an (5)_________ bus trip. The problem is if your routine changes a lot—if you go to bed at 11 p.m. one night and then at the (6)_________ of dawn the next. This can sometimes happen to people who do a lot of on (7)_________ work as they often have to (8)_________ some sleep during the day. This can be bad for their sleep pattern and sometimes, their general health.

Idiomatic expressions

5 Choose the correct options to complete the conversations.

1 A Dan told me you saw a bear when you were on vacation in Sweden.
B Yeah, it was amazing. It really stopped us dead in our *shoes / tracks*!

2 A I love having a cat. It sounds silly, but she's really good company.
B Well I suppose friends come in all *forms / shapes* and sizes!

3 A Should we go to the beach tomorrow?
B Yes, good idea. We should *make / put* the most of the good weather.

4 A We're going to Toulouse for our next vacation.
B Really? *Do / Take* the time to visit Albi, too. There's a great museum there.

5 A Has having children changed your life, Marija?
B Absolutely. Now that I have the girls, I *see / look* things in a different light.

6 A I had a real "aha" moment at work today. I was really pleased!
B Yeah, it's really satisfying when you *have / see* a flash of inspiration like that.

Vocabulary Extension
Further idiomatic expressions

6 Match the idiomatic expressions in bold in 1–6 to definitions a–f.

1 I got an e-mail from an old classmate today completely **out of the blue**. I hadn't spoken to him for years! ___
2 Don't buy souvenirs at the airport. They **cost an arm and a leg** there. ___
3 We're not sure if we're going on vacation or not. Everything's **up in the air** at the moment. ___
4 We only caught the train **by the skin of our teeth**. The doors were closing, but we managed to jump on! ___
5 Deciding which is my favorite memory is **easier said than done**. There are too many to choose from! ___
6 I was planning a surprise birthday party for Rita, but she found out. Charlie **let the cat out of the bag** by accident! ___

a tell somebody something that was secret (by mistake)
b be very expensive
c from nowhere, without expecting it, without warning
d something that sounds easy but is actually difficult to do
e with very little time remaining
f unconfirmed, not yet decided

7 a Complete the sentences with expressions from **6**.

1 A I'm really disappointed with these photos; they don't look good at all.
B Well, taking good pictures at sunset is ____________ .

2 Laura hadn't told anyone that she was pregnant, but I ____________ by mistake. I sent her a message on Facebook to say congratulations!

3 A Did you have a good time in China?
B Fantastic! The best part was sailing on the Yangtze River, although we only caught the boat ____________ .

4 We have tickets to the soccer final, but they ____________ . We can't afford to go out for the rest of the month!

5 A Is it true that you're going to Bhutan next summer?
B I hope so, but it's all ____________ at the moment. I need to find out whether I can get a visa.

6 My boss has given me a promotion! I wasn't expecting it at all; it was totally ____________.

b 12.1 Listen and check your answers.

Bring It Together

8 Correct the underlined mistakes in the text.

Nightlife in Puerto Rico

At (1)dust, we got into our canoes and followed our guide out onto the lagoon. Paddling the canoes was (2)easy said than done as the water was really rough, but ahead of us we could see an (3)awe-inspired view of the hills near Vieques. They soon disappeared into darkness.
It was the (4)death of night when we finally stopped paddling. Everything was dark and there was no moon in the sky. Then it began. At first, it was just a flash of light in the water. Soon, the whole lagoon was a cloud of bright blue. We couldn't (5) belief our eyes as the water shone with an amazing light, generated by tiny underwater creatures. I just kept looking and looking at it. I wanted to (6)take the most of it because it was so beautiful.
We got back to the beach at the (7)begin of dawn, exhausted and amazed. It was a (8)one in a lifetime experience and the best moment of my trip to the Caribbean.

A great piece of work, Ahmed! There are just a few mistakes. Could you please correct them?

1 ________ 2 ________ 3 ________
4 ________ 5 ________ 6 ________
7 ________ 8 ________

GRAMMAR
Reporting verbs

1 Choose the correct options to complete the conversations.

1 A What happened when you spoke to Martin?
B He agreed *helping / to help* me arrange the expedition.

2 A Why are we leaving at dawn?
B The guide advised us *setting out / to set out* early because it gets very hot in the afternoon.

3 A We were waiting for your phone call all afternoon!
B I do apologize for *not calling / not to call* you.

4 A Who was that man?
B He claimed *being / to be* a tour guide, but I didn't believe him.

5 A What happened when the police spoke to those pickpockets?
B They denied *doing / to do* anything, and the police just let them go!

6 A Why were you angry with the car rental company?
B Because they blamed me *for damaging / to damage* the car!

2 Look at the text messages. Rewrite the sentences in bold using the words in parentheses. Keep the same meaning.

1
I'm sorry I forgot to call you earlier! Talk tonight? xx
I apologize for forgetting to call you earlier! (apologize)

2
The meeting went really well —**my boss told me I gave a great presentation!** 😬
______ ______ ______ (congratulated)

3
Do you want to come sailing this weekend? **Dad promised that he'd take us!**
______ ______ ______ (agreed)

4
Denise and Sam would like us to have dinner with them. Are you free on Thursday? X
______ ______ ______ (invited)

5
Nikos said we should go to the movies tonight. What do you think? Carl
______ ______ ______ (suggested)

6
Just went to buy a newspaper... **The salesperson thought I'd stolen it!!**
______ ______ ______ (accused)

3 Complete the text using the correct form of the words in parentheses.

Last Friday a man came to my apartment. When I answered the door, he explained that he (1) ______ *(be)* a police officer. He showed me some photos of a woman. I had never seen her before, but the police officer insisted that she (2) ______ *(live)* in my apartment building. He said that he (3) ______ *(have)* some official documents with her name and this address on them. I apologized for (4) ______ *(not/be)* able to help him. I recommended (5) ______ *(talk)* to my neighbors, in case one of them had seen the woman.

The next day, one of my neighbors came to see me. She warned (6) ______ *(me/be)* careful because someone had robbed her apartment the night before. She asked (7) ______ *(me/help)* her, and I agreed (8) ______ *(answer)* some questions from the police. When the police came later that day, I suddenly realized something. The man who had visited me the day before had never shown me his badge.

Review: perfect & continuous

4 Choose the correct options to complete the sentences.

1 Aaron *is working / has been working* nights since March.
2 Sara fell off her bike when she *had ridden / was riding* home yesterday.
3 I can't see you on Thursday evening because *I'll have worked / I'll be working* then.
4 I woke up at the crack of dawn because *I'd set / I've set* my alarm for the wrong time!
5 *I've tried / I'm trying* to get in shape at the moment so that I can go hiking later in the year.
6 Let's go out. *We've been sitting / We're sitting* indoors all day.
7 By seven o'clock last night I felt exhausted because *I've driven / I'd been driving* since dawn.
8 *We'll have done / We'll be doing* all our assignments by the end of January.

5 Complete the web chat with an appropriate form of the verb in parentheses. Use perfect or continuous verb forms.

MarliesW says:	Hi Vic, how's it going? Excited about your vacation?
Victoria321 says:	Definitely! I (1) ________ (really/ look) forward to it. I (2) ________ (work) night shifts for the past few weeks, so I'm exhausted.
MarliesW says:	Yeah, you really deserve a few days off! ☺ Have you found somewhere to stay?
Victoria321 says:	Well, we (3) ________ (not/book) anything... until last night! We (4) ________ (think) that we would just find a campsite when we arrived. But I (5) ________ (look) online last night when I found a lovely campsite near the beach, so we decided to stay there. It looks really peaceful. By the time we've spent a few days there, we (6) ________ (forget) all about work!
MarliesW says:	Sounds great! Well, we should meet for a drink sometime this week. It would be nice to see you before you go. What about Thursday evening?
Victoria321 says:	Sorry, can't do Thursday; I (7) ________ (work) then.
MarliesW says:	Oh yeah, sorry! ☹ Why don't we meet on Friday afternoon, then? Go for coffee.
Victoria321 says:	OK. Let's try the new Italian cafe on George Street. I (8) ________ (want) to go there for ages.
MarliesW says:	Perfect! See you there at 4:30?
Victoria321 says:	Sounds good. ☺ Sorry M, I have to go... Shift starts in 45 mins! See you Friday! x x x
	Victoria321 is offline.

Bring It Together

6 Complete the blog post with one word in each blank (*isn't*, etc. = one word).

Mom's Blog World – Yuki Kamimura

Simple pleasures

Before I became a parent, everyone warned me (1) ________ it's really hard work. Even when they were congratulating me (2) ________ becoming a mother, people were saying how difficult my life would be. They told me, "In a few months you won't remember what it feels like to sleep all night long. You'll (3) ________ dreaming of being able to get up late." It's true: taking care of a baby is exhausting, but it's also lots of fun!

My daughter, Satako, is two and half now. Today, we (4) ________ just been laughing all day because her uncle and aunt are here. They arrived yesterday, and they can't believe how much (5) ________ grown and what she can do! When they last came, she (6) ________ learned to walk, but now she's running around everywhere.

When people ask me (7) ________ explain how it feels to be a mom, I just tell them that it's all about these simple pleasures: spending time with family and living in the moment. Before I had Satako, I'd (8) ________ working long hours for many years, so now I really enjoy being with her and sharing her excitement about all the new things she's experiencing. It makes you see the world around you in a different light.

FUNCTIONAL LANGUAGE Showing interest

1 Complete the words to make a conversation.

A How was your weekend?
B Well, not very good! I had to go to the hospital on Saturday!
A Hospital? What (1) h________ ?
B Do you really want me to tell you?
A Yeah, (2) g________ on.
B Well, I was chopping some vegetables, and I cut my finger.
A You're (3) j________ !
B I'm not. There was blood everywhere. I had to call an ambulance.
A You (4) d________ !
B What else could I do? There was only me in the house!
A Ah, poor (5) t________ !
B Anyway, I went to the hospital...
A Go on (6) o________ .
B Well, that was it. I got to the hospital, blood all over my shirt, and I got six stitches!
A (7) N________ way!
B It's true! Look!
A Ew! No, I don't want to!

LISTENING Activating background knowledge

1 a What do you know about the event in the photo? Prepare notes about the questions.

1 What event does the photo show?

____

2 Where can you see it?

____

3 When can you see it?

____

b 12.2 Listen to two people talking about the event. Check your answers.

STRATEGY Sometimes you can use your background knowledge to help you understand difficult listening texts. Before you listen, think about what you already know about the topic and ask yourself questions about it.

2 Listen again and complete Anna's notes. Write one word in each blank.

Stuart went to see the aurora borealis in (1) ________________ .

He didn't see it on the first night because it was too (2) ________________ .

Stuart said that the lights reminded him of a (3) ________________ fiction movie.

The aurora borealis is named after the Roman Goddess of the (4) ________________ .

The lights are usually (5) ________________ or green.

The best times of year to see it are (6) ________________ or spring.

STRATEGY When you have to complete sentences, follow the instructions exactly. Don't write too many words! Remember to read your sentences afterward to check that they make sense.

WRITING Checking your work

Hartnell Hire – Venezuela

★★★★

Young couple – Chloe and Ian

Neither of us has a driver's license, so we decided to rent some bikes to explore the beautiful island of Isla Margarita, off the coast of Venezuela. Luckily, we found Hartnell Hire, a little bike shop that rented us bikes. It's a fabulous way to explore this island paradise!

The store itself is easy to find in the main tourist area of Palomar, near Avenida Santiago Mariño. The island is very mountainous, so we rented mountain bikes that cost $10 a day. You need to leave a deposit of $50, which they return at the end of your trip. They will ask to see each rider's ID card or passport, but you don't have to leave it with them.

The bikes we rented were in good condition. The company also gave us helmets and gloves, although the helmets' straps were a little old and they were difficult to adjust.

The store owner, Carlos, was really friendly, and he gave us a lot of information about the island's bicycle routes. On Day 1 we went up into the mountains, and on Day 2 we took the more gentle path along the beaches and through the local fishing villages. It was a great experience, although the routes' uphill climbs were so steep that we had to get off the bikes and push them. We should have listened to other people's advice: some of the routes aren't recommended for beginner cyclists, like us!

All in all, we definitely recommend Hartnell Hire. There was only one problem (which is why we haven't given them a top rating). When we returned the bikes, there was nobody in the store. The store hours were supposed to be from 5:00 to 8:00 p.m., but we arrived at 5:00 and had to wait for almost an hour before Carlos's assistant finally arrived.

1 Read the review. Number the topics 1–6 in the order that they are mentioned.

a ☐ the equipment
b ☐ whether they would recommend the service
c ☐ what the actual activity was like
d ☐ what kind of people wrote the review
e ☐ the store's requirements
f ☐ why they decided to do the activity

2 a Read the review again. Underline examples of apostrophes (').

b Complete the chart with examples from the review.

We use an apostrophe to...	Example
show a contraction.	*It's*, (1) ________
show possession. • After a singular noun we add *'s*. • After a singular noun or name that ends in *s*, we can add *'* or *'s*. • After a plural noun ending in *s* we just add *'*. • After a plural noun that doesn't end in *s*, we add *'s*.	 (2) ________ (3) ________ (4) ________ (5) ________
Remember! We don't use an apostrophe with *it* to show possession.	*Its hours were...*

3 Think about a time when you used a service or did an activity, like the one in the review. Take short notes about your experience, using the notes in **1** to help you.

4 a Write a review of your experience.

b Check your work for mistakes. Make sure you have used apostrophes correctly.

STRATEGY When you write, it's important to use punctuation like apostrophes correctly. Always check your work carefully for mistakes.

PROGRESS TEST 4

GRAMMAR & VOCABULARY (25 points)

1 Rewrite the sentences using the word in bold. Do not change the word given. *(10 points)*

0 We're visiting the accounting department tomorrow.
We'll be visiting the accounting department tomorrow. **be**

1 Vincent won't be the architect of the new stadium. Lara also won't be the architect.
______________________________ **neither**

2 I was working for hours. Then I decided to have a break.
______________________________ **been**

3 Mr. Lukas was the physics teacher. His classes were in the old science lab.
______________________________ **whose**

4 Carol's still riding. She started at the crack of dawn.
______________________________ **since**

5 We had never tried the experiment before. The results were a complete surprise.
______________________________ **having**

2 Circle the option that doesn't work. *(7 points)*

0 I think I'll buy this *(aluminum)* / *cotton* / *nylon* shirt.

1 Our software company is sure to be a success. If you invest in it, there'll be *capital* / *some profit* / *a return* for you.

2 I'm worried about my business because we have a lot of *debt* / *grants* / *loans* to repay to the bank.

3 My sister refuses to use any products made from or produced by animals like *leather* / *mahogany* / *silk*.

4 Sophie's *flash of inspiration* / *drawback* / *breakthrough* came after she had looked at the results of the experiment.

5 They designed this gadget to be *lightweight* / *slim* / *touch-sensitive* to fit in your pocket or a small bag.

6 Bats usually appear in the evening, so the best time to photograph them is at *daybreak* / *at dusk* / *in the twilight*.

7 The views of Niagara Falls are *absolutely* / *completely* / *very* breathtaking.

3 Complete the sentences with the words from the box. There is one word that you don't need. *(8 points)*

breath call done figure fork get rubber ~~run~~ shapes tracks

0 Can you go to the store? We've *run* out of soy sauce.

1 The problem with these budget airlines is that you always have to ________ out extra money to pay for your luggage.

2 We've bought a red ________ bone for the dog to play with. She loves it!

3 I can't ________ out what's wrong with my computer.

4 Getting this project finished on time is easier said than ________ .

5 Our trip down the Amazon was spectacular. It took my ________ away.

6 I've been awake all night, so I really need to ________ some sleep.

7 Cell phones these days come in all ________ and sizes.

8 As soon as we turned the corner, we just stopped in our ________ . There was an awe-inspiring view of the mountains, right in front of us.

READING (25 points)

1 Choose the best title for the text. *(3 points)*

1 Our four-legged friends will show us the future
2 Nature is the mother of invention
3 Nasty in nature... but lovely in the lab!

2 Decide if the sentences are true or false. *(12 points)*

1 Cockroaches can eat products that are made of a kind of paper. ________

2 The bodies of insects are sometimes more complex than a human's. ________

3 Dr. Guha has asked the government to officially recognize his invention. ________

4 Dr. Frank Fish was inspired by the tail of the whale. ________

5 Lotuses die if they are in a very dirty environment. ________

6 Dr. Barthlott copied the smooth leaves of the lotus. ________

3 Complete the sentences with the cockroach, the whale, the lotus or none of them. *(10 points)*

1 ________ inspired gadgets for entertainment.

2 An invention based on ________ will help create electricity.

3 An invention inspired by ________ could be used to decorate your house.

4 An idea based on ________ was used to improve an existing invention.

5 ________ has inspired an invention that could save someone's life.

Where might the next big scientific idea come from? Surprisingly, it might be hiding behind your stove or growing quietly in the midmorning sunshine. That's because more and more scientists have been drawing their inspiration from the world around them. Nature is the new big thing, and it's been given a name: "biomimicry."

Cockroaches. They're everywhere. They can eat almost anything, even cardboard. Experts believe that they could even survive a nuclear war. We may think they're ugly horrible small black pests, but maybe we should be following the old advice; "If you can't beat them, join them." Having realized that cockroaches are super-survivors, Indian scientist Sujoy Guha invented a new artificial heart based on a cockroach's. A human heart has four valves to control the movement of blood but a cockroach's has thirteen, so it's a much stronger organ. Guha has already applied for a patent for his invention.

Inspiration can come from the big as well as the small. One day, the aptly named American scientist Dr. Frank Fish was walking around an exhibition when he noticed special shapes on a model of a whale. They were on the fins, the parts that a whale uses to move. He thought that they had made a mistake because the fins should be smooth. Having spoken to the designers, he learned that the model was accurate. These shapes on the fins help the animal swim more quickly. Suddenly, he had a flash of inspiration. Copying this design, he created enhanced wind turbines that generate more energy.

Biomimicry isn't just a question of copying animals. Dr. Wilhelm Barthlott noticed that although lotus flowers grow in very dirty areas, their leaves are always clean. He discovered that they are very rough, and this encourages dirty water to fall off them. After four years of research and development, a German company has now developed a paint that replicates this effect, using his ideas. It never gets dirty!

So it seems like the secret to the future is to imitate nature, but remember, it doesn't always come from the most beautiful plants and animals. New ideas can come from anywhere—even under the kitchen sink!

LISTENING *(25 points)*

1 T4 Listen to a radio interview about a trip to Petra in Jordan. Decide if Malikah likes ☺ or doesn't like ☹ these things. Circle the correct answers. *(18 points)*

0	Petra	(☺)	☹
1	Jordan in the Indiana Jones movies	☺	☹
2	traveling by jeep	☺	☹
3	prices in Jordan	☺	☹
4	the tourists in Petra	☺	☹
5	the weather in Jordan	☺	☹
6	the tour group that she went with	☺	☹
7	riding on camels	☺	☹
8	the tents in the Bedouin camp	☺	☹
9	talking on the radio	☺	☹

2 Listen again. Answer the questions. *(7 points)*

0 What time is the radio show broadcast?
It's broadcast late afternoon.

1 What does Malikah say about the temple in the rock?
______

2 How long should visitors spend in Petra?
______

3 Why does Petra suggest getting a guide?
______

4 What is the best time of day to visit Petra?
______

5 What does Malikah warn people to do?
______

6 How did Malikah hear about the Bedouin camp?
______

7 When did Malikah really enjoy the view of the desert?
______

WRITING *(25 points)*

1 Complete the survey with one word in each blank *(5 points)*.

Nightwork Survey – City Paints Inc.

Last week, we sent a questionnaire to all members of the workforce. Here (0) *are* the results of the survey. We found that (1) ______ three-quarters (80%) were happy with the present arrangements. (2) ______ vast majority of people said that the factory was a safe and friendly working environment. All the teams said they were happy with the night-shift system, (3) ______ one exception: the delivery department complained that their shift begins at 3 a.m. One of our (4) ______ interesting results was about the staff breakfast. All night workers said that they enjoyed this moment at dawn when everyone takes a break together. People were also happy with the safety arrangements, lighting and heating when the factory is in operation all night long. (5) ______ conclusion, it seems that the factory is well organized throughout its 24-hour operation, so we should give credit to the management for their hard work.

2 You have a job at an IT college. The new students have just completed this survey about their computer habits. Write a survey report using the information below. *(20 points)*

Link Up Computer College – New Students survey

Male: 17 *Female:* 16

US: 7 *China:* 9 *India:* 1 *Mexico:* 2 *UK:* 4 *Canada:* 6 *Switzerland:* 4

Preferred Browser – Internet Explorer: 21
Google Chrome: 11 *Safari:* 1

Operating System – Windows: 32 *Snow Leopard:* 1

Gadgets owned – Laptop: 33 *Tablet (iPad, etc.):* 15 *eReader (Kindle, etc.):* 3 *Blackberry:* 0

7.2, p. 46, Exs 2 & 3

1 **A:** Hello there, ma'am. How can I help you?
B: Please can you tell me when my visa will be ready? I've been waiting here for nearly three hours.
A: I'm very sorry, but I can't answer your question. You'll have to wait until one of the visa officials can see you.
B: I'm afraid that just isn't good enough. I need to know what's going on. If this isn't straightened out quickly, I'm going to have to make a formal complaint.
A: OK, wait here one moment, please. I'll try and find out what the problem is.
B: Thank you.

2 **C:** Oh no, I don't believe this!
D: What's happened? What's in that envelope?
C: They've sent my tax return form back... again! But I'm sure I filled everything out correctly. It took me hours to straighten out the problem the last time they returned it. I really don't have time for this! Why do they make these forms so complicated?
D: Look, don't worry, darling. It's probably just a simple mistake. Let's sit down and look at it together. If you get all the documents ready, I'll make us coffee. We'll figure it out.
C: OK, thanks Richard.

3 **E:** Good evening, sir. May I see your ticket, please?
F: Oh, of course. Here you are.
E: Thank you. And sorry, but would you mind turning your MP3 player off, please? This is the quiet car, so we ask passengers not to use cell phones or listen to music. There is a sign here.
F: Oh, OK. I'm sorry, I didn't realize. I didn't know what the sign meant.
E: That's no problem at all. If you'd prefer to listen to music, you could move to another car. It's up to you.
F: OK, thanks.

4 **G:** Excuse me, officer. What's going on here?
H: There is a gas leak inside number 24. It may be dangerous, so we're asking everyone to wait outside until the problem has been solved.
G: What? But my office is inside that building. I have an important meeting in an hour. I need to go inside and prepare!
H: I'm very sorry, but I'm going to have to ask you to wait here. Engineers from the gas company are dealing with the problem at the moment. I'm sure the work will be finished within the next hour.
G: Sure. And what am I supposed to do until then? Honestly, this is just ridiculous...

8.2, p. 52, Exs 1 & 2

1 **A:** Have you seen Mary? We're supposed to be having a meeting about the Jaycott trial.
B: No, sorry. By the way, have you heard that she's leaving?
A: Really, when?
B: Next week apparently... Mm, that reminds me, she borrowed some money from me last week. I should get it back before she goes.
A: Good luck with that! She's so forgetful.
B: Huh, yeah. Incidentally, if you do see her, can you remind her that we're going out for dinner this evening?

2 **C:** Guess what? I'm going to be in court next week. I'm on a jury.
D: Oh really? That should be interesting.
C: Yes, I think so. It's a fairly long trial though. I had to take two weeks off work.
D: Talking about trials, did you see the report about vandalism on the news last night?
C: No, what happened?

3 **E:** OK, I've finished my report on the burglary at the school, so I'm heading out now.
F: OK, have a good evening. Before I forget, can you come in a little early tomorrow? We have a lot to cover.
E: All right. I'll try to be here by 8. Changing the subject, have you heard if there's a date for the arson court case?
F: Not yet. I'll let you know as soon as I hear anything.
E: Thanks, that would be great. OK, I should go. I don't want to miss my train. See you tomorrow.
F: Bye!

8.3, p. 52, Ex 1

Ladies and gentlemen, may I have your attention, please? Due to vandalism on the railway line, trains will not be running from Baltimore to New York this morning. Passengers for the 9:35 service to New York should wait in the station parking lot for the replacement bus service. The buses will depart at about 10:15 and should arrive in New York at about 12:00. Trains from Baltimore to Trenton are not affected. Please see signs in the station for more information. We're very sorry for this change in our services, but the problem was only discovered this morning by the local police. We hope that all services will be back to normal by late afternoon.

9.2, p. 58, Ex 1

1 **A:** I'm sorry sir, but I can't let you into the swimming pool without a swimming cap.
B: What do you mean?
A: It's a rule. You have to wear a cap in the swimming pool.
B: I don't believe this! I've just walked for thirty minutes to get here, and now I can't get in!
A: We do sell them, sir. You can buy one in the store.
B: All right. And how much do they cost?
A: Only $1.
B: Fine. I'll do that then.

2 **C:** Hello?
D: Hello , am I speaking to Mariam ... Ahmadi?
C: Yes, who is this, please?
D: Do you have Internet access at home, Ms. Ahmadi?
C: Look, I'm...
D: If you are interested in changing your Internet service provider, we can offer you a special price for the first six months.
C: I'm very sorry, but I'm not interested...
D: We can install WiFi throughout your home within 24 hours of signing your contract.
C: Sorry, but I don't want to change my Internet service! This is the third call I've had today.
D: Our offer is extremely competitive and if you would...
C: I'm sorry. I'm not interested in all these deals. Good-bye.

3 **E:** What's up, Sam?
F: I just checked my lottery numbers online. I use the same ones every week...
E: Oh right. Did you win anything this time?
F: No such luck. I would have won $50, but... I didn't buy a ticket!
E: Oh no! Why not?
F: I went to the store yesterday to buy a good luck card for my little sister. She's taking her university entrance exams next week. I was going to buy a lottery ticket at the same time, but I completely forgot.
E: Poor you!

4 **G:** Hey Joe, what's wrong?
H: Someone stole my skateboard.
G: Oh no!
H: The thing that makes me really angry is that it was another skateboarder who took it. I left it in the street to answer the phone. It was a place where lots of us go skateboarding. It wasn't at school or at the sports center or somewhere like that. It's so annoying!
G: Was it worth a lot of money?

H: Yeah, it was very valuable. I won it in a competition at the skate store.
G: Oh, poor you. That's so unlucky.
H: Yeah, and now I'll have to get a job so I can save up for a new one.

T3, *p. 61, Exs 1 & 2*

Good evening, and welcome to *Police Report* where we keep you up to date with crime in the local area.
First of all, we have the arrest of four protestors who tried to enter the nuclear power station illegally on Sunday night. The protestors, all between 17 and 19 years old, argue that nuclear power is untrustworthy and dangerous. The police released them on Monday without further charges.
Residents of New Town have taken action against vandals in their area, following a series of criminal acts. Stores, bus stops and even apartment buildings have all been damaged in the last month. A new law has been passed that allows the police to give anyone committing this type of crime an immediate fine of between 50 and 100 dollars. Next, a warning to anyone out there who downloads movies from the Internet. The government can now stop Internet access for anyone using pirate websites. Bear in mind that police will only give a single warning before stopping the Internet connection. Around 300 connections have already been closed. Police have now confirmed that no one was injured in yesterday's fire at Good Hope High School. However, the school believes that it will need to spend over $10,000 to repair the damage caused to its indoor tennis courts, where the fire was started. The principal said that she was "very disappointed" by the irresponsible behavior of the students who started the fire. Finally, a funny story to start the weekend. An unlucky thief named Roger Churchill chose the wrong house to rob last Tuesday night. While Churchill was stealing the DVD player and the TV, he was caught by the house's owner, Mr. Bruce Twining. Mr. Twining is an ex-professional boxer, and he held Churchill in the living room until the police arrived. Churchill has now been sentenced to eighteen months' community service. That's all for now from *Police Report*. Keep your eyes open and stay safe.

10.1, *p. 63, Ex 8*

1 A lot of food and drink packaging is made of polystyrene.
2 The old temple downtown is made of beautiful white marble.
3 Copper is often used to make electrical wire.
4 Bottles of wine or oil often have tops made of cork.
5 There are too many ugly gray concrete buildings in this city.
6 The walls of the villa are decorated with painted ceramic tiles.

10.2, *p. 66, Ex 1*

When you're shopping at the mall do you fork out a lot more money than you expected? Do you know which products are the biggest rip-off? Today we speak to retail specialist Huang Wen, who'll tell us how to save money shopping.

10.3, *p. 66, Ex 2*

A: Huang, welcome.
B: Hi Pamela.
A: So Huang, what are the biggest rip-offs at the mall?
B: Actually the biggest rip-off often comes before you get to the mall, especially if you have to come into town. The price of train tickets changes a lot during the day, and there are a lot of special deals, too. But often the staff at the train station don't tell you about the offers.
A: So how do we get the best prices? Look online?
B: No, it's actually best to call the station to find the cheapest train tickets.
A: OK... And when we get to the stores, what should we look out for?
B: Er... the sales! The price you pay for clothes, for example, is usually several times their real value. It's best to wait until the sales to buy them.
A: But there are never clothes in my size in the sales.
B: If you want to buy something on sale, you have to go on the first day. Ask someone in the store what day the sales begin. Here's a tip: sales often begin on a Thursday when most people are at work.
A: Right, OK, I'll remember that. What other products are overpriced?
B: Imagine the scene. You've been shopping all day for a new leather sofa. You've found neither the right color nor the right design. You're exhausted. So what do you do?
A: I usually go to a café with my friends.
B: Exactly, and this is where the real rip-off happens. How much do you pay for a cup of coffee? $3?
A: Yeah... Something like that.
B: Yes. Well, the real cost of the coffee is about 10 cents a cup! So what are you paying for?
A: Well, the staff I suppose... and the big shiny coffee machines...
B: That's true, but with a 1,000% profit the café soon pays for all that!
A: OK, they're making a lot of money, but I don't want to give up my coffee!
B: Neither do I, but shop around. Local cafes usually offer cheaper drinks than the big chains.
A: OK, Huang, thanks for your advice. Now if you'd like to call in and ask Huang any questions, our number is...

11.2, *p. 72, Exs 1 & 2*

A: We've all been there... There's something wrong with your computer, and you can't fix it. You phone for help, and... Many of us have had frustrating experiences with computer helplines. But how does it feel on the other end of the phone? Today on Insiders, I'm talking to an ex-call center operator, Nikhil. Welcome to the program, Nikhil.
B: Thank you.
A: So first of all, how did you get your job in the call center?
B: Well, the job came from nowhere, really. I studied computer science in college, and one evening I met this guy outside the library on the campus. He gave me a leaflet from a call center. They were looking for computer science students to work for their IT helpline.
A: So you got in contact with them?
B: Yeah. I was just the person they were looking for. I could work evenings and weekends, I knew about computers... Oh, and most of all, I was happy to work for very little money because I was a student!
A: And how did you stay motivated? It must be very boring.
B: Actually, the work was pretty stressful! In the call center, there's a computer on the wall and it tells you how many callers are waiting. It also tells you how long each call lasts. So, everyone in the office can see exactly how well you're doing, all the time!
A: Hmm, that does sound stressful! Did you get along with your coworkers?
B: Absolutely. They were all really lots of fun, and my boss was laid-back... unlike the customers! Some of them were really difficult, and others asked really silly questions!
A: Like what?
B: Um, well, one person called up because of a problem with his handheld games player. He was really angry because he'd only bought it a week before, and it had stopped working. After half an hour, we discovered the problem—he'd never recharged it. Honestly, you can make your technology as intuitive as you like, but some people will never understand it! Another lady said she couldn't install a certain program onto her computer... After twenty minutes, we found out the problem... She hadn't bought the program and she didn't have the disk!

A: Really?
B: One person told me he couldn't boot up his computer. I told him what to do, but nothing worked. Finally, I asked, "Is your computer on? Have you turned it on?" And he said, "Oh, I need to turn my computer on, do I?"
A: How do you stay calm in situations like that?
B: To be honest, I just thought about the money! I was a poor student, remember? And most of the time it was funny. In fact, it was useful because now I work for a software company. When I'm designing software, it's useful to know about the problems people have with technology!
A: Nikhil, that's all we have time for. It's been great talking to you.
B: And to you.

12.2, *p. 78, Exs 1 & 2*

A: Hi, this is Anna speaking.
B: Anna, hi, it's me.
A: Stuart! Great to hear from you! How are you doing? Where are you this week?
B: I'm in Tromsø, in Norway.
A: Oh yeah, you're writing a feature about the aurora borealis, aren't you? Have you seen them, the Northern Lights?
B: Yeah, we saw them last night. It was amazing, a once in a lifetime experience.
A: Hmm. It's a hard life being a travel journalist, isn't it?
B: Yeah, well... Um, actually, Anna, I need your help.
A: Oh, OK. What's up?
B: I need to write my blog for the magazine website, but... my laptop's broken. I can't get it fixed until the weekend, and there are no Internet cafés here!
A: You're joking! What are you going to do?
B: Well... I was wondering... Can you write the blog post for me? Just this once.
A: Oh Stuart ... Well I suppose, if you can't get to a computer... Let me get a pen and I'll take some notes... OK, ready.
B: OK, so I'm staying near the Sandvannet Lake in Norway, and we've come to see the aurora borealis. The first night, in the dead of night, we drove out into the woods. It was very exciting, but... unfortunately, we didn't see the lights because it was too cloudy.
A: OK... Carry on.
B: So we went to the woods again last night. And then... we finally saw them. These bright, moving lights in the sky. Honestly, Anna, it's breathtaking, like something from a science fiction movie!
A: OK. So why do they have such a strange name?
B: The aurora borealis? It's because they're named after Aurora, the Roman goddess of the dawn.
A: And what do they look like?
B: Well they're like waves of light in the sky. They're usually green or red, but I saw lots of other colors, too. I couldn't believe my eyes...
A: And, in the blog, don't you normally include some travel information for the readers? I mean, when can they see the lights?
B: Well, it's winter now, but the best times are spring or autumn... Look Anna, I'm really sorry, but I have to go. Thanks so much for helping me with this. You're a lifesaver!
A: Hmm, well, you owe me.
B: Definitely! Thanks again, and talk soon.
A: OK. Bye Stuart!

T4, *p. 81, Exs 1 & 2*

A: This is Jeremy Price. It's time for the last afternoon slot on travel tips. We're here with Malikah, who'll be talking to us about her recent trip to Petra, in Jordan. Malikah, welcome.
B: Hi Jeremy.
A: So what did you think of Petra?
B: It was fantastic. We all know the temple in the rock from photos and from the Indiana Jones movies, and you know the movies are good fun, but actually visiting Petra is incredible. It's an awe-inspiring place.
A: What is there around the temple?
B: Well, Petra itself is a very large site with many ancient buildings. To visit it properly, you need two or even three days.
A: And how do you travel around? By jeep?
B: No, that's too noisy for me. Instead, I suggest renting a horse!
A: A horse?
B: Yeah, you can ride all around the site.
A: Amazing. Now, what about guides?
B: Personally, I think it's good to get a guide. It's a great way to meet local people. And don't worry about prices—they're very fair in Jordan. You can get by on a few dollars a day.
A: I agree. So what's the best time to visit Petra?
B: Go at sunrise when there aren't many people there. It's breathtaking. Sadly, there are a lot of tourists in Petra now, and in the afternoon it's just too crowded.
A: And very hot, I imagine?
B: Yes, it can be incredibly hot. You should bring lots of water, whatever time of day you visit.
A: OK ... What about accommodation in Petra? What's that like?
B: Well, last time, I actually stayed in a Bedouin camp—I'd really recommend it. I found out about it online. I went with a tour group, and everyone was really friendly. Luckily, we didn't travel by camel or anything like that. I'm not a fan of camel rides!
A: So what was the camp like?
B: When we walked into our tents ... well, they were beautiful. And camping in the desert was amazing. If you looked out of the tent in the dead of night, you could see so many stars. The view was stunning.
B: Mm, it sounds like a once-in-a-lifetime experience. Well, Malikah, that's all we have time for today, but we'll be speaking to you again soon, after your next trip! Thanks for chatting with us today.
B: Jeremy, thank you. It's always a pleasure to come on the show.